GREEN CARNATIONS
GLAS NA GILE

Editors

John Ennis
Moxie Lofton

BOOKHUB©

P U B L I S H I N G

Published by Book Hub Publishing, An Independent Publishing House, Galway & Limerick, Ireland. www.bookhubpublishing.com
Copyright Editors (2020)
The individual contributors assert the moral right to be identified as the authors of their own work.
ISBN: 978-1-8383142-1-7

Moxie Lofton founded Queer Writers of Ireland with the goal of bringing like-minded individuals together and creating a community of creatives. They studied English and Philosophy at UCD and have a focus on storytelling and interpretation. While they do write, their main focus is facilitating creativity and promoting creative expression. Practical writing aside, Moxie loves spending time learning about narratology and theories of creative writing. Their other creative outlet is music, including guitar and bass.

John Ennis is a writer, poetry anthologist, and editor, with twenty-one publications to his credit to date. Retired from Education, he moves between his adopted Waterford and native Westmeath. He continues to espouse causes — his work is often polemic —and he has been green starred by Amnesty International. He believes in *World Without War* and tries to live up to Yeshua's Beatitudes. His *Later Selected Poems 2000-2020 Going Home to Wyoming* is published by Book Hub Publishing, Athenry, Galway, Ireland.

Introduction

Green Carnations, Glas na Gile, compiled and published in 2020, is an anthology of verse from twenty-five contributing LGBT+ poets on the island of Ireland.

The book charts the ups and downs of first loves, longer partnered relationships and sexual encounters.

If "the heart is a lonely hunter", the poets featured know the terrain.

Theirs is a country where the motley of individuality is struggled with and worn. No tiresome sameness in the verse, but, at their best brave lines and voices heard and felt at the raw nerve of human existence, what it means to be human in an LGBT+ context. One that is as old as and older still than the creatorly plains of genesis.

The poets are gathered by their first names, or initials, and range in age from the late teens, –some in their final Leaving Certificate Year 2020 – to the thirties. The same-sex Irish Marriage 2015 Referendum passed by a majority of the electorate (celebrated in some poems) is a line in the sand to be lived with, accepted and celebrated.

Each poet was requested to contribute a short biography and to introduce the poems. Some poets prefer to use a pseudonym. Some accompany their poems with artwork. All struggle with identity, who they are. Individuality rather than editorial sameness is reflected where possible.

Sometimes something of a sharedness of serenity is achieved. More often than not the growing pains, loves, endearments and durabilities that are anyone's in a relationship.

The book is essentially a young person's anthology, a sharing among contributors and with readers as all face a common future.

CONTENTS

Achia Dounia

My writing has always been a direct reflection of my life, the highs and of course, the lows. In recognition of my sexuality though, a lot of my work has been based on whom I would consider to be the love of my life, and on the flip side of that rather positive work, I write about my sexual abuse history and its impact. As an individual who grew up in a sexually/domestically abusive home by cause of my father, my sexuality was always hidden, which my Arabic background also enforced. And when I came out as gay, my sexuality became a "consequence" of my tragic childhood, in a societal view. My current partner was the first person I told about my abuse, and in turn, she changed my life by the courage she inspired in me. It would be my biggest ambition to one day have a book published in appreciation of her.

Consent

Your fingers are like shovels
Scraping my reaches for honey that
You cannot produce
You await my music like it belongs to you
Pulling my strings
Daring to manipulate lyrics
From this tuned out mouth
And when you don't hear approval
You mistake my silence
For nothing
Because you heard the aching in my heart
You heard the crying escaping my lungs
You've seen my eyes
Begging for justice
And you never, once
Stopped.

Self-intolerance

You surrounded yourself
With people who hated themselves
And in turn you forgot how to love this body,
This heart
You resented the limbs that wrapped themselves
Around you during the hardest part of the night
You dismembered the skin
That protected the bones
That you allowed to become hollow

Remember that soul
That so graciously takes your
Lack of consent
And continues to burn gold,
Every morning like the sun
Holding hope that you will,
In time,
See that there are rays within you,
Too.

Raw

Maybe we'll fall in love again,
A slow approach,
An enigma barely noticeable
A quiet laugh,
A tidy tuck of hair
Behind an ear
Eyes peering into another's
Curious, and knowing
Nothing like the fireworks,
The hellfire burning in our hands as we unleashed flames
Onto each other's skin
The passion that was red,
angry
Corruptive
But addictive
Compelling, and there was not one person
That we completed each other
So manically,
So correct.

The "social" platform

What did you think?
Those photographs represented what?
How I indulge so deeply in my happiness and here
I am laughing and here I am
Appreciating my body
I did not spend five hours at 7am
Trying to decide which one exaggerated my greater assets
By your standards

And in which angle
Can you see the brilliance of my mind?
Did I let on that behind that mass of
Over exposed skins are broken bones?
Will your words of approval
Heal them too?

Platonic playground

How high did that swing go?
Up past the brambles of your mind, that mess?
Was your heart as bare as those trees,
Did the leaves fall heavy,
Like my footsteps
Crushing the life out of autumn

What brought the winter, Daddy?
When did you decide the heat
Wasn't good enough?
What determined that cold

Why did you let go of my hands,
Why did you tie them?
Why did you take back that crown,
The one you gave me?

Why did you point out
One rose in a park full of weeds
And tell me that was me,
If you only intended to pluck my petals
Clip my wings
And ensure me,
Little birds weren't capable of flying.

Her

These tar-filled,
Froth-corrupted lungs
This dark destroyed soul
Eyes that have seen dead bodies in her reflection
Body moulded by the opinions
Of lesser bodies
Has become consumed by the riches
Of your ability to love so carefully
That this heart
Has been broken
And reconstructed
Tamed,
And come alive.

Adam Cooper

is an aspiring writer from Offaly, Ireland.

From a young age, Adam has been interested in literature, often found buried in a book or trying to write his own. He is hoping to become an English teacher so he may share his enthusiasm for English with young minds.

Recently, Adam has been focusing on writing poetry, although he also writes the occasional short story.

His collection of poems maps out the progression of young love and the impacts it can have on a maturing soul. It highlights the fiery beginnings and ultimately the sombre ends. Above all, the collection is a celebration of the many lessons learned throughout such a crazy time.

Extra Seasonal

You never gave me butterflies in my stomach
 they were in my heart
 flying higher than they'd ever been before. . .

Champagne love
intoxicate me with your gaze
let me languish in your strawberry haze
pour me a glass of second chance
let me steal another dance
let me re-live your glorious sound
pick me up from the pounding ground. . .

Burn me
with your starlight love
sear my skin and boil my blood
blind me
with your silhouette glow
make me new and break my bones
scar me
with a history of you. . .

Do you remember
when we split the moon in two
a piece for me, a piece for you
both rocks kept like a promise
last night my rock rocketed back to the heavens
and I had to wonder
whatever did you do
with your half of the moon. . .

The ghosts of your kisses
riddle my flesh like hidden tattoos
your breath on my neck
                              lingers
like a forgotten thought

phantom fingers interlock
                    with mine
while the gift of your smile still haunts my mind. . .

Your hands are cupped round my lighter –
The wind is howling like a ghoul. . .

The wind blows on the windows
A crackling rattle, shattered reflection
on our place, our space . . .

Darkness /ˈdaːk.nəs/ the absence of light

Heartache /ˈhaːteɪk/ the absence of yOu

I scare away most of the birds
so spend my days
crucified by duty
on the golden fields

illuminated by our once infinite moon
ever a reluctant guardian
to ageing cornstalks

my hay-filled head it
dangles day after day
looks down on the coos
where woodquest feast

I'd like to cut loose
tempted with the angst
of august cuckoos
and hit the skies

Aoife O'Connor

is a writer, musician and teacher. In her career as an educator, she has encouraged her students to express themselves through writing. Students have responded to this by developing a passion for poetry and stories, with some particularly talented students winning national creative writing competitions under her tutelage. She is now focused on putting that passion into her own writing. Aoife lives with her partner and their two beagles in Dublin.

This collection of poems was written in response to the unique experience of growing up and having relationships in the midst of the fight for marriage equality in Ireland. The instinctive pull towards women even while being in a straight relationship is explored in the poem 'It Doesn't Feel Like That When It's Her' as well as the world-tilting lows confronted during heartbreak in poems such as 'Gone' and 'Like Fire and Gunpowder'. It is a grouping of poems that detail the experience of love at different stages of life as a gay person in Ireland.

These experiences were only possible because of the members of the LGBTQ community who were fighting for their right to love for generations prior. The brave work done by those in the community and how that has allowed Aoife to embrace her identity, is acknowledged in the final poem from this collection, 'Difríocht'.

Gone

I feel within memories.
Maybe I was in a one man show,
Perhaps it was only an empty stage,
With her as my audience.

It seemed so easily exited.
With me still singing,
My heart bleeding on the floor,
Beating to the echoing sound of a slammed door.

Like Fire and Gunpowder

Love is patient, kind and slow,
Tread down that path if you've wit to go.

The thing I felt was sharp and fast,
Vice-like in its deathly grasp.

It Doesn't Feel Like That When It's Her

We had a beautiful thing,
You and I.

Our shape mirrored the pairings on TV,
Luring me in to the peace of the ordinary.

My mind became a body,
My body became putty,
Moving and responding to the want in your hands.

One whisper of a girl's name,
Wrenched me clean from the double-sided tape
We had wrapped around each other.

The surface layer torn away,
Revealing an ancient lulling pull.

Her advantage was evident immediately.
Animal instinct trumped rational thinking
As we paged the sheets.

Each song encroaching, and finally
Encompassing, all that we had made.

It Can Be Done

You can bend where you once broke.
The hardened sinews of your heart can soften,
To pump bright oxygenated life.

You will laugh harder than the last time.
You now know the value of humour.

Vulnerability won't be the commodity it was before.
Tears of mirth and sadness will spill as often as rain,
Embraces given every time,
No power will be gained from displays of pain.

Wilted weeds can be pulled from the soil,
And flowers planted in that same spot
Will burst with blossoms on the 14th of May.
It can be done.

Love

It's not the romantic dinners,
Nor the proposals.
It's not even the first kiss,
Or the first touch,
Or gasp.

It's the constant presence.
When one of you would rather be elsewhere,
And you choose to be here,
Just to be there,
For them.

Gratitude is a Fickle Fox

Darting from view only to appear
suddenly, standing stock still
amber coat ablaze, filling your vision
when you nearly lose someone or something
you're grateful for.

Sometimes, it's a moonflower
uncurling and shining, when the boastful sun melts,
and a humble and marred orb takes its place.
When you meet someone with less than you have
and they thank the universe every day for their riches.

Gratitude can come like lava,
erupting from the solar plexus,
in the reflective monotony of driving,
hands enjoying the warmth of the steering wheel.
The weights of your soul balanced:
Love, health, purpose, autonomy.

It's never in the winning, or the trumping of others
that gratitude shows us its face.
It's in the rare moments when everything is going right
that each gift we have been given
illuminates like drifting fireflies in the dark.

Difríocht

I held my difference close to my chest,
Cradled like a baby bird.
Its wings all matted,
From the matter in its speckled egg.

I had been hatching this difference,
Since I was young.
Small fingers cupped the warm oblong shell.

Gentle with it, but sometimes,
Cruel and neglectful.
Allowing the egg to be ignored.

The warmth seeping out, nearly killing it
Before, because I could not bear to leave it,
Carefully embracing it again.

It hatched without warning.
At first it frightened me.
How can I keep you alive?
How can I feed you?

Then I thought of all those,
That had hatched before.
Some had survived even with no seeds,
And no nesting place.

Wings clipped.
Or if the bird had grown and taken to the sky,
A hunter's bullet had ripped it,
From the air.

Gentle hands,
Had nursed the difference back to life.

Nourishment was given,
Guns unloaded.

It was the birds that flew before,
That paved the way for mine to soar.

Chandrika Narayanan-Mohan

is a Dublin-based arts manager and writer from India, who has also lived in North America, Sweden, Turkey, and the UK. She has been featured on The Moth and Mortified podcasts, with work aired on NPR and Irish radio. She also regularly performs at literary and cabaret events in Ireland. Chandrika was selected for the Irish Writers Centre XBorders programmes in 2018 and 2020. Chandrika's poetry is included in *Writing Home: The 'New Irish' Poets* from Dedalus Press, and her work has been published in *The Honest Ulsterman, Poetry Ireland Review,* and *Banshee*. She recently won third place, and was highly commended, in the Fingal Poetry Prize 2020. She is the first ever guest editor of Poetry Ireland's *Trumpet* literary pamphlet, and book reviewer for Children's Books Ireland's *Inis* magazine. By day she is Marketing and Development Manager for Fishamble: The New Play Company. Twitter: @ChandrikaNM, Instagram: @Chandrikanm.art

An Introduction

Hi there,
Allow me to make an introduction.
I am smiling because I can highly function
On wounded birds and spark-plug repairs
These are the cogs turning, going spare
When I hand you my business card and instil confidence.

The work I touch turns to gold
And I don't have to be quiet about it so
I shout, I shout, let it all out
Because work is the thing I can't do without,
Because it makes feel me worthy, and wanted
And loved by strangers,
Because the dangers of real intimacy
Scare me way more than accountancy.

So why can't I, map-minded
Apply the formula for a business life
To me? Find like-minded
Individuals who make me feel
At home in my self, to
Co-achieve, co-love, co-produce
Friendship, what a collaboration that would be
A grand production, hey! Look what we made, isn't it great?

I want to show off how I feel right now,
But then I guess it's a performance,
Not an internal re-evaluation, a counting of stock
An inventory that is being ticked off,
Box by box, I want to
BE WELL, in ALL CAPITALS,
So I can be in YouTube Videos about how
I Won Against Depression

Go me! See? If I can do it
So can you, thumbs up, wink,
Hey kids, don't do drugs (unless you really want to).

So where is my certificate of
Trying Hard? I want a handshake
Every time I don't hate myself,
A pat on the head when I clean a single dish,
A thank you for not being abusive today
Would be great, thanks, take your time
I'm here all day, not… going anywhere
No it's fine, it's all in my head, I…
Breathe. Traffic sign stop.
I want to swim in a calm of my own making.
I want to take bad news without shaking,
Or smoking 8 cigarettes in one sitting,
And crying myself hoarse, unslept, unkempt.

I want a brain as organised as my desk
With a to-do list I can tick off
Where I can chart my progress, mapped,
Monitored, reported,
Quantitative results
Organised alphabetically, sorted,
But instead it's just a series of palpitations
That tells me that today isn't ok
And an absence of swollen eyes that tells me that today is.

Today. Is.
It exists. And the number of times I tried not to.
When I planned my way to a watery grave
Where the black turquoise freeze
Squeezes me out of my own room,
I would give myself to the land that fed me sadness
And I would be part of your sand,
Getting everywhere, stuck in people's pants
As a last revenge from the afterlife,

All the times I felt like an inconvenience,
At least this time it would be on purpose.

But goddamn the fight in me,
The low hit points but the urge to battle.
I was never built to quit, but built to be hit
Repeatedly, by circumstance, and my own fist.
Still battered, still stitched, my patchwork-quilt heart
Still beats, sometimes too loud,
Sometimes barely,
And sometimes, rarely, it beats just for me,
And when it does I smile at the world,
I really do, and there's that streak of dusty sunshine,
That tells me, today, it's fine,
And thanks, I'm fine,
How are you?

Cured

The summer exposed me,
My sweat, zip-heavy down my chest, peeling back skin,
Displaying hot steaming innards.

Summer left me hanging off hooks
Like a freshly-butchered pig,
Fat sizzling in the heat.

It was not the season of fruit bearing,
Of quiet buxom bites into sweetness that gives,
That fulfils,
That nourishes
That composts gently at the end of the garden.

Instead, I fermented,
Meat-slick, citrus-slimed,
A fresh agony made black around the edges,
Made fuzzy with parasites,
Aged, cleaned,
Monitored, and consumed.

Emily

She types, 'I miss you',
An echo across an aching ocean,
Where all there is to say
Trembles through the silence.

Engine of Love

I am an engine of love.
I am steeped in fumes from the spluttering
The muttering
And all the false starts.

I have fed myself a fuel of regrets
And insecurities that bite, and rust
That stiffen, but now I must
Somehow, ignite myself
Into existence.

I have wires and veins
And they're clogged with sadness
And an inward crumbling
Stumbling over a mess of detritus
Shattered from a stronger, beta version
Of myself.

I spent a long time with wires crossed and screws loose,
A heart coated in the dust of neglect and disuse
And every extended length of copper
Was left disconnected, nothing conductive to curl onto,
Nothing electric to flow through.

But I have visions of pistons:
Black-slick and oil-thick,
A locomotion of emotion, raring to go,
Because I've stopped up every exhaust I could have used
To dispel this toxic ooze
In my throat, shuddering into palpitations
Oh what a sensation it would be
To feel an ease of connection.

So here, take this key,

Oil up this tin man and start me up,
Baby I need lubrication
Because the imagined sensation of white-hot action
Is too much for these old metal plates
That have contracted and shrunk from the cold.

I want love to shimmer in the air around me
This smile is going to be a sunshine machine
You've never seen anything like this!
I shall churn out magic with my fingertips
Touch and glow, it's going to be hot,
And I want everyone to be caught in this spin
Because in the state I'm in,
My core will be rotating faster than the speed of light
And any moment now, I just might Burst into life.

Clodagh Mooney Duggan

is an emerging poet. Born in Wexford in 1992, she has since become a writer, actor and director. Originally training as an actor, she graduated from *The Gaiety School of Acting* in 2013.

Since graduating, she began to write for the stage, her most recent credits include **Made from Paper**, which premiered in Dublin 2020 in **The Scene and Heard Festival.** **The Women Who Loved Me & The Women Who Couldn't** was her first published poetry collection, which was published in **Poethead** in March 2020.

Clodagh Mooney Duggan - This collection, **The What-ifs,** is a selection of poems which look at the struggle which occurs when a person sees their life split into two paths. The path they are currently on, and they path they could have chosen. It is designed to represent how vulnerable we are as humans, and how we are all searching for love, or something to give meaning.

At its bones, **The What-ifs** is an exploration of love, and self-destruction.

The Greeks

I give you a promise,
Perhaps a misleading one.
Strolling behind you on an frosted evening
Comparing old Greek myths to our love.
"We are the new lovers,"
I say.
"We are writing a new language."
I feel wings fracture my spine and prepare me to fly.
"We are, something special."

In front you are silently weeping.

The Homemaker

I have taken to making candles,
And bread,
And threats.

"Come home"
I say.
"Home to your wife."

The words fall from my lips and harden on the floor.
I hear the line clink on her end.
Gone.

"Come home"
I say.
 "To the whiskey on the counter.
The knives scraping off plates.
Records dimly playing what sounds like Christmas music."

I have taken to making desserts
And bath salts
And mistakes.

What do you reckon jail feels like?
Is it this?

The I love you.

Coldly I turned from the steel,
The mechanics of a thing
That hasn't been explained
But is known to us.

The curves of your back
As you stare out the window

"What are you looking for?"
I scream in my mind
As you turn around with cold eyes

Steely
And hard.

The moonlight strangles your hair
And I mourn the turning of the earth
From the sun.

Stillness roars,
I trap myself in a shake
Untangling an impossible wire.

"I love you"
She whispers
Holding the truth back in her tongue.

Unwittingly a tear falls from her eyes
The move from stone to water
"I love you"
I say

Grasping her wrist
I'm lying

The fairy-tale

Falling
From a whisper.
A boy stares out the window
Making wishes
Of
Buried treasure
And swords.

What happens when the snow
Fades
And the twigs
Meet their destiny?

The stars inside him,
Are coming together
To tell him a fairy-tale.

The Quest

Staring at an empty horizon,
Reaching for the memory of a lost map.
Directions are
faded
Steps, uncertain, are retraced.

Maybe

I had a compass,
Once.
The needle forgot its purpose.
It smiled,
Knowingly,
And pointed to the West.

Blindly I wandered on.
Searching for the X,
That was moved.

Finding myself outside a derelict house,
Windows murky with dirt.
I called for you.
But I had forgotten your voice
When someone called back.

The Almost.

There is a beauty to the element of wanting.
The neat,
Simple,
Desperation of it.

I found it in your eyes.
Piling cards of memories and mementos on top of each other.
What was I to you
Do you reckon?

Less than a notch,
I would wager.
But a challenge.
Or something challenging.

Threatening to unearth the sadness
You would sometimes hint at
But would never discuss.

I think of it often
More than I suspected.
The map on your wall
And the pink light that sometimes illuminated a love in your eyes.

Or

Something

Close to love perhaps.

Grasping like children
Who have learnt all the emotions they care to
Rejecting all new ones that feel alien.

I'd write,
But I wouldn't know where to send the letter.
And the pen fractures in my palm
When it graces the paper.

I did, I think, love you.

And I'm sorry for that

David Fallon

is an Honours English Bachelor of Arts student at Waterford Institute of Technology. Writing poetry since the age of fifteen, he submits work to various publications and anthologies. He was recently published in an Anthology Remembering Palestinian Victims of Occupation; *Turangalîla-Palestine*, compiled by Ennis, J. and Mallaghan, D.

The following three poems articulate the "queer" writer's experience. These queer poems turn feelings into emotions personified through a brook, fine wine and us. The poems show that the queer writer has always had a voice with the same depth of passion for love, that has been the thematic concern of poetry throughout the ages.

The poem "Beside the babbling brook of dreams," a take on "the babbling brook", poeticism of the 18th C., recalls a pivotal moment with a lover beside a brook. Little did both lovers know the passion they felt for each other. The poem gathers pace as it is set to the rhythm of a beating heart. The poem finishes with the lovers caught in an embrace unaware of their depth of emotions. Will they kiss or not?

With "Us" the speaker contemplates "U" the letter, the word and the former partner it signifies. The poem descends into anarchy as the relationship between the speaker and "U" falls apart like the sentences within the poem. Ultimately, we question if this unhealthy, toxic and dangerous relationship is salvageable or if it is better for these two to part ways for good.

"Golden Delicious," a poem and testament to a dead lover, begins with descriptions of the partner in repose. The poem breaks as the speaker descends into a trance like state due to intoxication. The speaker remembers and dreams, vividly, of his queer lover's sensuous energy. Unable to cope, he longs for his lover. The poem is a metaphor of the experience of drinking wine, emphasising addiction, love and how they are entwined.

Beside the babbling brook of dreams

That boy I know,
When did he get so complicated?
Dancing by the brook on his own,
How he has grown!

With a magnetising appearance…that's physical –
he prances and skips moving as one,
in unison with this narrow rivulet,
– and just as I contemplate this frolic with the brook,
with nature –
he pirouettes, mystifyingly fixed in the same spot.
Gradually as my eyes gaze;
amazed I no longer see a man,

Instead he becomes an immovable yet steady force.
 Like the brook,
　　　　　– 　slow and steady carving the earth
　　　little by little…
　　　　　– 　his presence makes me tremble
as gurgling white noise fills my senses.

Yet beneath that translucent surface
LIES a world unexplored and a nature
… stark … that no one dares to venture
stormy winters turn this harmless trickle into a river swell
capable of untold destruction.

Nonetheless, strolling down this stream of consciousness,
– his naturalness is beautifully untamed
since it was a rill.
Growing and maturing from all its channels,
now heading down stream.
The current waves goodbye
and I left wondering if I'll see it again

breezily fresh and sparkling…
The brook echoes, a bubbling sound
low and flat,
as a man sits wounded,
who has lost his heart?

Yet I wonder,
in all curiosity,

sitting among crimson leaves as trees whistle
singing to one another. A perfect chorus…

For us

as the babbling brook glistens and softens now,
under gleaming silver moonlight,
breathing sensual crisp air.
Are we dreaming…staring
into each other's eyes – Mystery
catches us by surprise
it sets our minds… mine… racing.

This man?
This dance.
That kiss—
Our brook
Bliss

Us

The letter **u,** used
through text; spelt
YOU, choose
a meaning?
what is…
the significance of **U**?

This plain *auld* simple letter
conveyed through drastic
subtle word play…
or innuendo
suddenly –

Out of the blue; **U**
shift… **I** stagnate…
joy becomes obscured,
the sentences and the meaning becomes lost and torn apart by a tender
massacre of **us**. Of
structure
blood black as ink stains a pure canvass. The reality is lost
yet the pen like a knife reigns upon the page,
– a tiger's tyranny tears through the innocent lines.
It's now **I** begin to question – the intention of **U**
 – the future of **us.**
Our differences preserved,
we are not k-noun by another name, my single individuality…
U lacking refinement – our feeble vulgarity
　　　　　–the possessiveness of **U**.
　　　　　And **I** bound by no rules and convention... Yet even now
　　　　　I have yet to find a formula that works,
　　　　　Or an insanity that –
　　　　　appropriately fits **us.**

Golden Delicious

Delicate fruit,
Deliberately selected –
Oak aged and "resting" – typical
I savour that scent!
Of an eloquent Irishman,

               –his modern testament

a delicate sentiment of what
is truly elegant.

Captured and pressed,
the skin now pale –
lemon yellow.
Green glints shimmer,

a warm honey colour?
As far as I remember.

Innate characters sooth my senses…
the tantalising sips,
the drying after taste…
the lychee smells…

Your beautifully smooth texture

Oh what a dream it would be!
to dive into the depths of you.
What treasures do you hide –

How many have dived and survived?

Sweet
Spicy
Crisp mouthfuls
seep from me to you

Our sexualities tune
our sensual aromas blend.
time and space blur.
Nostrils Flare —

Your Odour.
Your Colour.
Draw me in.

I become ensnared
enmeshed in you.
Gravitating towards you.

No one has returned.
Your wish is my command!

Bound...
my destiny lies in your hands.

Diarmuid Fitzgerald

was born in 1977 in Co. Mayo and grew up in Co. Cork. He lives in Dublin. Two collections of haiku have been published by Alba Publishing, *Thames Way* in 2015 and *A Thousand Sparks* in 2018. A chapbook of poems *Camino Cantos* is forthcoming from Lapwing Press. He has completed a collection of poetry called *The Singing Hollow*. Poems have appeared in *The Stinging Fly, Cyphers, Crossways, Crannóg, Boyne Berries, the Blue Nib, Impossible Archetype, Flare, It's a Queer City: All the Same, an Anthology of LGBT Writing from Limerick, Teachers Who Write* anthology, *Mustang Bally* anthology, and *All to One Side* anthology. A poem won 2nd place in the Ballyroan Library Competition 2018 and in 2020. Diarmuid won an Individual Artist Bursary 2018 from South Dublin County Council. Sixteen poems were highly commended in the Blue Nib Chapbook Contests IV and V in 2019. See www.deewriter.com for samples.

Diarmuid Fitzgerald – Some of these poems came from the Marriage Equality referendum campaign 5 years ago. I was a canvass leader in my own area. The referendum campaign was a life changing experience for me, for the LGBT+ community and for Ireland. Three years after the campaign I started to write poems about it. I guess it took that long for the poems to percolate through. Poetry is a slow art and it resists being rushed. When poetry is rushed it comes off badly. Seamus Heaney spoke about this when he resisted writing poems on the latest atrocity. I now know what he meant. The poems gathered here are from a collection in progress called Rainbow Street. They are about LGBT+ themes was well as personal fitness, love and personal growth. All of this may change over the next few years as I work on them.

The Rose Garden

We walked hand in hand though Inchicore
to the War Memorial Garden,
sunken beside the road.

The roses came up to our waist,
boxes and boxes arranged in a circle
divided by a central grass plane.

There was a stone wall and pillars,
a plaque said something like 'remember'.
I recall your kisses, the way our lips met,

how we imprinted the grass with our bodies.
I placed my legs between yours
and you held me in a tight embrace.

I smelled roses, cut grass
and dandelions. No birds sang
but they could have for all I knew.

My heart soared, floated above
and I saw the pattern of love
criss-crossed in the paths.

St. Stephen's Day

I meet my childhood friends in Charlie Mac's Bar.
We exchange polite gestures.
I stand at the edge of the circle, a little crowded out.
We talk of the latest match, who is engaged,
and the price of houses.
I am unanchored here.
Whether I would return here, break up with my boyfriend,
or settle down is simply beyond them.
I am a tourist in my own town.
I will find my family elsewhere among those whom I do belong.

The Pressures of Love

for Ishmael Marquez

And then you and I slept naked.
Your chest against my back,
the hairs electrifying me,
your heat came into my body.
You played with my earlobe,
slid your arm under my arm
and stoked one of my shoulders,
drew your hand down my chest,
I felt your manhood against me.
There was no gap then.
I turned,
kept your look
and the pressure of your body on mine.

Count Day

I
The white ballots spill from the boxes
with the buzz of counting. I tried not to miss a single tally.

I was exhausted by pounding the pavements
like being on a gym treadmill with the speed turned up.
I drove a cute guy from my team to his home.
He had a lovely beard and a kind face. I hoped
we could start dating but nothing happened.

Down at the local church there were
girls and boys in their holy communion dresses.
The snow of their clothes filled the estate.

II
Later I got the bus into Dublin Castle,
the nerve centre of celebration.
Rainbow flags festooned the square,
with loud and cheerful music echoing
through the heart of the city. Dame Street
filled with men and women of all ages,
dancing on the street, laughing and singing.

A man stood there, with his placard
demanding that gay people repent
and live a life according to the Bible.
A crowd surrounded him and chanted
"Love heals all." He ran away.

To celebrate I found a place at a bar. A lady
thanked me for all my dead legs, bleeding toes.
She could not have stomached asking people
to allow her to marry her girlfriend.
My heart swelled with pride.

III
By nightfall I was with my friends
drinking cocktails. I felt like a full citizen
of this country for the first time.
An Indian summer came early.
We lit white paper lanterns.
They floated up and away
under the woolly clouds.

Origami Skin

to Ryuichi Okamoto

I
My Japanese boyfriend
said my skin was like origami paper.
The pressure of his hand was a jolt of electricity,
the frisson of skin on skin.
We held our tongues together,
shared semen on and in each other.
He wanted whiter skin.
I wanted different hair,
to change my skin to a darker shade.

11
In Japan I learned to slur the 'l's and 'r's.
I picked out words from the streets signs,
round my mouth to say them right,
'exit', 'entrance', 'up' and 'down'.
I appreciated the sheen on a lacquer screen,
admired a traditional tea cup,
held a fan the right way.
I knew the local ways
and yet there was still a gap.

III
I missed the umbilical cord
to my motherland,
so loose it could unravel.
I wrote home,
felt the pressure of the pen
marking its message.
I folded the letter and posted it,
asking them to send news,
and without using its name
to spell out love

Jogging in the Sun

In this ice-cream weather
my shoes hit the ground,
feel like they are running under me.
The lampposts move by slowly.
My tongue is a dry field
and my skin tingles as sweat covers my forehead.
Fear bubbles up in me. A jumble of worries
comes to mind. I keep this rhythm up,
release each thought with the pounding.

I take a sip from my bottle,
the magic of water
cools me from within.
This day all things are right
and in their proper order.
The sweats dries away as the sun beats on,
sparks flash on passing cars
and the traffic sings. My thirst slackens.
I feel the glitter of hope as I run home.

Eoin McEvoy

is an amateur visual artist and poet who works in the Irish language. His poetry explores queer relationships and desire. He is a member of the LGBTQ+ artist collective *Aerach.Aiteach.Gaelach.* and the Irish-language network *An Queercal Comhrá*, which strengthen the Irish-speaking queer community through social gatherings and spread awareness of queer Irish language arts and histories. Eoin is a past winner of the Craobh Aimhirghín poetry competition, one of the Literary Competitions of Oireachtas na Gaeilge.

Eoin McEvoy – The first two poems here explore the subtle, sudden shifts in queer desire. 'Fuckboy' is a charged poem which probes the emotions attendant to non-romantic sexual relationships. The narrator's uncertainty around the wisdom of continuing one such relationship quickly gives way once sexual contact is made and his desire crystallises. Through the prism of the sexual act, he is refracted into seemingly unconnected body parts in ecstasy before the climax is reached with the shutting of an eyelid as a shield against the potential of a romantic connection. As the two bodies merge into one, the narrator's desire explodes into colour and the poem closes, as it begins, with the recurring uncertainty and loneliness that descends as soon as the heat of the encounter fades.

'Gnéisc' is one of the poet's Luas poems and has as its defining structure the narrator's sense of smell. On a balmy day in the belly of the Luas, the narrator encounters a sweating stranger whose smell disgusts him. After a moment, the narrator catches amongst the other odours the note of a fragrance he recognises and is overcome with an urge to interact physically with the stranger. The poem's ambiguous final word leaves the nature of this urge open for interpretation, mingling the sexual with the violent, and the transient moment of focussed awareness on the tram is suddenly plunged into the narrator's sense memory and questions around the history which produced it.

Fuckboy

geallann do mheabhair duit
iar bhfuaradh a shíl

nach dtitfidh tú choíche
dá eangach arís

ach taibhsíonn sé romhat
is iarrann cead luí

agus deir do bheál tá
thar an níl i do chroí

do mhian ina criostal
a chorp ina léas

ag ionsaí do phriosma
go ndéantar díot siosma

ligeann tú uaill
ó lasmuigh de do bhéal

do mhalaí ar foluain
do chromáin san aer

trí pholl do chluaise
cloistear scairteanna do bhéil

is aithníonn d'inchinn
gur sea iad go léir

líontar do chéadfaí
le cumhracht a chnis

is líontar do chuas

go dtí nach leat tú ach leis

trí mhac imrisc do shúile:
a ghnúis ina sleá

nó go ndúnann tú duille –
sciath ar an ngrá

gan cheangal na rosc
sibh ag tuairteáil d'aon toirt

do chuid ingne ina chraiceann
seanfhios agaibh beirt

go spréifear do dhath
ina bhogha go fial

ach go bhfágfar leis féin é
iar bhfuaradh do shíl

***

Fuckboy

("a clunky translation")

your reason vows
once his seed cools

that you'll never fall into
his net again

but he appears before you
and asks to lie

and your mouth says yes
over the no in your heart

your desire, a crystal
his body, a ray

assaulting your prism
until you schism

a cry bursts out
from beyond your mouth

your eyebrows float
your hips aloft

through the hole in your ear
come words from your mouth

and your brain recognises
a yes in each shout

your senses are filled
with the scent of his skin

your pelvis is filled
till you belong to him

through the pupil of your eye
his face, a lance

till you close the lid –
a shield from love's glance

with both eyes closed
you thrust as one

your nails in his skin
as you both well know

that your colour will be spread
in generous pools

but he'll be left alone
once your seed cools

Gnéisc

boladh –
feoilmheall fir
faoin ngrian
a bhí á bhá
i mbolg an Luas

allas an lae
tiubh i gclúmh a ascaille
é lán málaí sceallóg
gréisc na geire
géire an fhínéagair

Agus do chumhrán leis

bhí dúil agam
a chraiceann
a bhualadh

uaidh

Gnéisc

(a rough translation)

a smell –
a meatball of a man
under the sun
drowning him
in the belly of the Luas

the day's sweat
thick in the fur of his armpit
full of the stink of bags of chips
the grease of fat
the cut of vinegar

And your aftershave too

in me an urge
to beat
his skin

from him

Dobharchú

dobharchú ar leac
ag faire na linne
ar fhaobhar na hoíche
ag fiach

ar chuar a shúl
leacht an luain
piléar de mhac imrisc
ag fiach

gan chamóg gan fuaim
mar scian tríd an scáthán
síos leis san uisce
ag fiach

geiteann sé roimhe
mar airgead beo
trí bhroinn an tsnámha
ag fiach

an poll roimhe dubh
le searc, le seilg
isteach leis sa slua
ag fiach

thar riastradh na leannán
a ngéaráin i ngreim
i mbaill seirce a chéile
ag fiach

ag aclú a choirp
timpeall seanchú liath
sa tóir ar na cuáin
ag fiach

an dobharchú ag seilg
gan stop gan stad
a shúile guail lasta
ag fiach

is feiceann sé aisling:
a chorp ba ró-álainn
leis féin á phiocadh
ag fiach

Otter

(a translation for comprehension)

otter on stone
watching the water
on the edge of the night
craving

on the curve of his eye
the milk of the moon
his pupil a bullet
craving

no ripple, no sound,
a knife through the mirror
down through the water
craving

he ripples along
like liquid silver
through the womb of the pool
craving

the darkness is brimming
with love, with chase,
he joins the drove
craving

past the wrestling lovers
with canines embedded
in each other's love-spots
craving

flexing his body
past a grey waterdog

pursuing the pups
craving

the otter continues
no stop, no rest,
his coal-eyes lit
craving

and he sees his *aisling*
his once beautiful body
alone, being picked
by ravens

Frances Wilde

is a 24-year-old writer from Nottingham, UK, living in Dublin, having previously lived in Galway. She has a BA in English Literature and an MA in Film Studies – Theory and Practice. Her poetry was recently read at the Irish Writers Centre WomenXBorders event and has appeared in Flash Literary Journal Lancaster.

Frances Wilde – My work is focused on spaces and a phenomenological perception of them, locating liminal identity in space. For example, reimagining the West of Ireland as an ominous, beckoning place; intimacy as exasperating; catastrophe as comforting. Many poems focus on the spaces of West Connemara. I completed an Artist Residency on Inishlacken Island in 2018 and 2019. fwilde@irishfilm.ie

Outskirts

Fixed myself
in an unassertive stance
in the Central Library Bar,

Perched precariously
on the peripheries of
conversations.

Opposite a couple,
talking in shades of
hilarity and comradery,

about their trip to England,
football, beer, Liver birds.

How peculiar Liverpool sounds
with Dublin vowels.

Dame Street to Hope Street –
GPO's aggressive seagulls
to bombed-out-Cathedral.

One small sea apart,
Home and home.
Each catching a glance with
the other in acknowledgement.

My dialect shaking hands with both.

Doom Lover

I spent five years
obsessed with doom.

I am a veteran of fear,
worst case scenarios,
and existentialism over
shoddily rolled cigarettes
in the Róisín Dubh.

I've catastrophised the
craziness out of myself,
prepared for this dystopia
in bed, insomniac nights

dowsed in epiphanies over
mortality.

I stopped growing when I was
fifteen – my mind closed in on
itself and the shell of
an imagined normality
cracked open, raw and bark-like.

When the world did end,
we became free.
Liberated from pretence,
populated with the
presence of death.

Behçet's Diagnosis, May 2018

Emergency room,
Dr. Chris with the
gorgeous hair,
Ten blood tests,
Infections and diseases,
Gynaecology, Rheumatology.
Grappling with chronology.

Antibiotics, antivirals.
Painkillers –
not strong enough.
I am
My mother,
Unable to admit defeat.

Too worried to remember
The important bits.
Temperature: 42°C.

Too tired to whimper
                    for help.
5 am, and we're
Up in the lift:
University Hospital Galway's
Saint Nicolas Ward, Level II.
Hilarious, looking back –
The fear of lifts
My main concern.

Catherine bringing
Too many clothes,
Full of love
But saturating space,
With reminders that

This was happening,
Not to a dissociated story
of a body, but to me.

Phone charger
Not reaching the bed.
The only entertainment? Helping
Bernadette with her crossword –
Freshwater duck: WIGEON.

Leaving on the fifth day,
To put on the washing machine,
Sleep for thirteen hours,
And take colchicine.

Our Foot's in the Door

That Guardian article read
time, space, money,
money for time and space.

Men love to talk
barriers and quotas,
Putting a percentage on
poverty.

Drinking filter coffee
and tapping the face
of a gold-plated watch.
Watching us squirm.

Our knuckles are
squashed mightily
in the door hinge.

Bruised and burnt-out
but unmoving.

We're at the threshold
Linked battered arms
Holding leaky pens.

Swim to Inis Leacan

I see myself
in the Gurteen Bay
shallow cove,
reflected back
a wobbly silver-blue.

Sombre clouds shrouding
a clear silhouette,
ocean washing in,
to tell me (in coercive tones)
who I am.

Memories rising
from the water
to greet me.

Who were we,
swimming for miles,
at slack water?
Arctic terns,
screeching cheerily above,
exude the end of a season.
Tide turns.

Jennifer Nolan

was born in 1992 and has spent the 28 years between then and now collecting a vast array of pets, writing lots of silly fantasy-based short stories and less silly, less fantasy-based poems. She hails from County Kildare, where she still lives and works in Animal Welfare. She's also terrible at writing biographies.

Her poetry tends to revolve around mental health, her experiences as an LGBTQ+ person, and a general sort of nostalgia. The selected poems are from a bit of all of these topics, written over the course of the last three years or so. . . . . .

A Visit to the Old Orchard

The apples are crisp
They crunch under our boots.
Fat calico cats doze in the corners,
And as we pass they skitter to their feet.

The red apples are the highest
We shake them down, into crinkling supermarket bags.
This orchard was bigger when I was a child
These trees I had climbed every one.

My summers were spent here
Climbing trees long chopped down
Canoeing from a jetty now rotted right through
We'd sneak out of church and roam here, wildling children till we were
called back for tea.

My friends I picture them as they were. Young with skinned knees and gap
teeth.
I haven't spoken to them in years.
We've all wandered back from Narnia
Back to a smaller version of our childhood.

Here, where a tree is just a tree. Where an Orchard is all it will ever be.

The trees are orange and yellow but trees are all they are now.

And I follow my father to the car, hauling bags full of the apples, back to
where they will be sweetened, stewed, and tucked into pies.
We go for coffee and little cakes and we talk about old friends, apple pie,
the way things were.
The things we lost
The things we found
The things we buried in the ground.

Mental Intermission

Under heavy covers I am free,
I sink to dreams that taste placebo-sweet.
The night it gives me peace I cannot keep.
They say sad people dream so very deep.

I wrestle sleeping hours from the dawn,
I doze on armchairs overstuffed or bare.
They tell me it's the pills that make me sleep.
They say sad people dream so very deep.

I'm lost in all the quiet that night brings,
Wherein my mind is silent and at rest.
No worries shaking in, or fears that creep.
They say sad people dream so very deep.

The world is far too loud and far too close,
It thunders and my heart starts missing beats.
But here I tune it out and count some sheep.
They say sad people dream so very deep.

Diagnosis

I rail against the rising and the setting of the sun,
 I hate the clouds and stars and all the roiling of the seas.
I curse the growing plants and all the flowers, every one.
How dare they all continue on when time has stopped for me.

 How dare they sprout and bloom and form and flourish lush and tall,
 When I am frozen solid in this moment on my own.
When nothing I can do will ease your pain or help at all,
When the world is full but I have never felt this much alone.

How dare the birds sing loudly like they have no heavy hearts.
How dare the rivers thrive and not know pain or death or fear.
 The word spins on and madly on, a thousand ends and starts,
But until you stay or go my friend, I'm frozen waiting here.

That's *so* Gay

And just what are you so upset for
You know I don't mean it that way
I only meant creepy or dumb weird and bad
I didn't mean YOUR kind of 'gay'
I just meant it's sappy or boring
Or dull or dramatic or fey
Or needless or stupid or plain old revolting
It wasn't offensive, okay?

First Love

Brown-haired girl with the lights down low
Come take my hand and we'll dance real slow
Tell me your dreams and your football teams

What makes you stay and what makes you go
Brown-haired girl with the hazel eyes
Call your mom, you can stay for the night
We'll steal the good booze, drink it all on the roof
And talk about life 'til the new sun's rise
Brown-haired girl won't you walk me home
Hand in hand to ward off cold
Gloves with no fingers where perfume still lingers

Jessica Anne Rose

Hello, my name is **Jessica Anne Rose** and I'm an 18 year old writer and aspiring musical theatre singer. Hopefully by the time this is printed, I'll be over in London studying musical theatre, if predicted Leaving Certificate grades didn't backfire on me. I identify as bisexual although I say I'm 80% gay at this point. My first feeling of romantic attraction happened to me when I was 12 on the school bus. I went to an all girls convent school. It was unexpected, though if you really look back at baby me wearing flannels and find my diary from when I was eight where I wrote 'I wouldn't kiss a boy for chocolate,' the signs may have been clearer. My pronouns are she/her. I've been writing my own stories and poems since I realised I could. I've never been shy about a topic and once scared my third class teacher writing about a corpse in a story set in the industrial revolution. I won a place in the Young Playwright's Programme held by Graffiti Theatre and had my play, 'Pushing The Pen,' acted on the Everyman Palace Stage during the 2018 Cork Midsummer's Festival. I am very proud to say it was an all female production, directed by a female, written by a female, with all female actors. It was in association with feminist icon Louise O' Neill's play adaptation of her novel 'Asking For It.' Nowadays I can be found scrolling on poetryireland.ie at 3am or writing parts for the novel I will get around to writing someday. . . . . .

I tend to use writing as a way of expressing the negative emotions I sometimes have, which is what you've ended up with for ¾ of these. I wrote **'tea talk'** over a year ago and my mom read it out to the gran aunts and they laughed so I kept poetry to myself after that. I wrote **'there is a bird'** one of the nights I couldn't breathe and was tired of experiencing such potent emotions over and over. And then I wrote **'the conch shell'** and decided to share it, if nothing else, to put my own spin on destigmatising taking medication for mental illness.

To try make you feel a bit better after all that gloom I threw in **'fizzy.'** It's a love poem that was awkwardly received.
….. I promise you I am a happy person.

overture

there is a bird

there is a bird that lives inside my chest.
it hunches for space behind my rib cage.
it is not a pretty bird or a romantic sight
it is nauseating to prevent it from its
natural, compulsive flight.
-

at nighttime sometimes it knocks a vein
and starts to shriek and flap about
it screams in pain to be let free
and bashes pointlessly against my bones
it's pain is mine and lives in me.
-

I sometimes cry of pity for the bird
I long to free it but it is sewn behind skin
it's beak is dangerously close and could
puncture my pulsating heart.
and so I leave it as I should.
-

In bed I listen to it rattle against my ribs
And look with damp eyes to the ceiling,
The ache follows me for days and weeks.
So I've learned to live with a bird in my chest.
I'm learning to process the ghosts of its shrieks.
-

But the bird has not quite slit my heart
So Hope and I still whisper sometimes
Of the day we'll teach the bird to fly
When my chest opens and the squawk of joy
I feel a flap of feathers and a tear reaches my eye.
-

I'll bear the scars of course.
I imagine tracing over them, explaining to
My children how much I've had to do to get here
I hope they will never understand it

And that their wings will spring up unclipped.
Hearts intact.

act one

the conch shell

- a poem –

when i was young my grandmother told me
to press my ear to conch shells
for a chance to hear the sea.
i never heard the sea, but i heard
the whistling of the wind cupping
its hand gently to the side of my face
whispering circular noises into my ear.
nowadays, i hear that noise at 9:45pm
when i swirl my pill bottle
and count the circles, one by one
into my mouth
to try to find that peaceful sound again.
19/9/19

intermission

act two

tea talk

Please make me a cup of tea

And you can ask me how I've been
Though clearly you've seen
The utter state of me!
Two sugars and milk will do it
Then let the mug sit
Let it stew for a bit
Take a minute and watch it.
See the colours swirl and lighten
Steaming up a face that's tightened
Even the teaspoon's tinkle will frighten
Me, would you care to be enlightened?
You see the last few weeks have seemed
Like you've added double the sugar I need
Or ran out of milk entirely
I mean the thought of black tea turns me green!
It's funny how the days where I want some more
There's just no milk left in the store
Or the days where I don't fancy a pour
Fifty people will ask me if I want five cups more.
If I had to tell you how this feels to lug
I'd need much more than this measly mug
I'm talking buckets, a huge jug
Throw in a warm hug?
Tea isn't just a winter thing
You'll find me sipping in the spring
Through exams, in summer, gets me through everything!
But sometimes the kettle just makes my ears ring.
Let the steam cloud up the kitchen
Let every table flower wilt
But why on earth would I be crying
Over milk that hasn't been spilt?
It's silly, I know,

Those flowers once again will grow
And I'll buy some more milk, you know!
We can forget this little shame show.

I won't have a cup of tea today.
The sweetness is just too much for me to take.
I don't know why my mind goes so far astray
In a matter of minutes! ....But I'll be okay.

Finale

fizzy

you are not like a flower that can be
picked apart petal by petal.
it is not that easy to get down to the stem!
many women are compared to flowers
delicate
soft
pliable
but you are not like any woman I've known
-

when i think of you i see gold.
i remember the first time I saw you and how you made the room feel full,
welcoming me with a crinkled eye smile.

we were both stone cold sober but I felt like I was full of champagne
bubbles
the kind you read about in books that taste like novelty and excitement
but you are not a novelty that wears off

then,
you laughed loudly and carefree, I glanced at you,
and that was the moment i saw you were gold.
-

you exist in a way that shortens my breath
because you are unapologetic,
confident and unprecedented,
beautiful and intelligent,
and you possess a hidden strength you shouldn't have to have but you yield
it like a sword and face it head on.
-

If this is to be a fleeting experience, let's remember it like an ill advised
moment of youthful insanity
remember the feeling of eyeliner gluing tired eyes together
the smooth bump of road heading home with music ringing in your ears
maybe a little alcohol pleasantly warming your chest as you float home,
with laughs ingrained into your skin along with spritzes of perfume

and the welcome promise of a warm bed.

-

Dear Cliona,

I could have read a library full of books and I would not have found
someone as special as you are to me.

someone who gives me so much hope that people like me exist in this world.

when this fog lifts and the world comes back to life,

please don't fear that my emotions will dissolve too in a puff of rose
coloured smoke!

-

they were there long before and will be long after, flashing with gold,
crackling with anticipation for the unknown

we both have parts of us we'd not anticipated having

but neither of us have ever let those parts limit us

-

so, when this storm passes, I will be here waiting with my hand outstretched
for yours.

I promise if you take it to always have an open ear to listen, a gentle voice
to advise,

a laugh for your jokes and a smile to remind you

 I am so happy I chose you and you chose me.

Leah Keane

is a native of Castlerea, County Roscommon. She graduated from NUI Galway in 2018 with a BA in English, German and Creative Writing. Unsurprisingly, she is now a barista.

Her work has been published in print by *Poetry Ireland Review*, *Skylight 47* and *The Stony Thursday Book*, and online by *The Poetry Village* and *The Mouldy Bike Periodical*. She has studied poetry under Alvy Carragher and regularly attends Galway's *Over the Edge* literary events.

Leah Keane – The first poem included in my series, **"Cars and Dismissal"**, was written during my poetry workshops at NUI Galway. It's a stream of consciousness of sorts that deals with my own sexuality, insecurities and family dynamics. Although much time has passed since I wrote the poem, very little of its confusion and longing has gone away. It's a bit too honest at times (sorry, Mom), but I'm proud and incredibly relieved to have written it. **"The Old House"** reflects on childhood memories from a more mature perspective. I don't often write with much intent – things just come out – so it's hard to break things down without giving myself too much credit, but re-reading it now, there's an odd air of mystery to the poem, which in a way, reflects how little we really know as children. To sum it up, the poem is about how notions of nostalgia can collapse as we get older and slowly become privy to information we were once too young to know.

I wanted to wrap up the series with a small dose of (much needed) optimism. Written pre-Covid, **"May I?"** expresses the urge for life to get started. For many people (young people in particular) it may feel as though life is currently at a never-ending standstill. This poem is a reminder to remain positive, productive, and considerate of others, especially in difficult times.

Thank you all for reading. Please enjoy! - Leah Keane x

Cars and Dismissal

Where some families have a dining room
to talk about big issues, the Keane family has the car.

Not one car necessarily, different ones
over the years, each one slightly less shitty than the last,

and the thing is
that you're in cars a lot,
so it could happen at any time really.

Maybe one trip you're just in the mood
to talk to your Mam about the fact that you love boobs.

Or a bit drunk, she's driving you home from the pub
and it slips out — that you really really like it when girls get their nips out.

You see the real thing is
that you don't believe in big issues
and you often talk in monotone,

so it's quite likely that this is how the conversation would go:

"Well."

"Well."

"Were ye busy today?"

"Ah. It was alright."

Seat belts on then silence for ten minutes.

There are some poorly kept bushes on a roundabout.

It reminds you of your own poorly kept bush.

"Mam, I think I'm gay." I don't think she'd mind.

One night she was drunk,
ended up coming home at around three o' clock.
I was in bed in my brother's room downstairs
because I thought I heard mice in the attic.

She was rummaging around in the kitchen for a while
before a phone rang, and habit called her outside
to pick apart the grind with a backdoor smoke.

Later she must have noticed
that an extra light was on downstairs,
so in she came and sat down
half on top of me by the edge of the bed.

And oh how she lamented.
She'd had a horrible lovers' quarrel
with her partner of nearly twenty years —
a retired *Eircom* installation man,
who loves taking her out to dinner on Strand Hill
and talking about his bladder and the neighbours.

And I said, "Sure you'll get back together."

"No, no. Not this time."

She let out a sigh.

"Promise me, Leah that when you get a bit older
you'll marry a nice, rich man who'll take care of you
and then you'll never have to work a day in your life.
A man…

or a woman, I don't care, as long as you're happy."

Of course they got back together two weeks later,
but those words gave me just enough
to make me feel secure.

The Keane family has the car for big issues.
Like that time when I was nine
And Mam told me that Nana was dying.

Out she came with it, in a calm, sympathetic voice, "Leah,
Nana's very sick and she's not going to get better."

I had been sitting in the back seat,
and when I started crying
she urged me to come crawl into the front
where she hugged me very gently against her
with one arm around my shoulders
and the other resting firmly on the wheel —
all the while she never stopped driving.

I'm not worried about being excommunicated,
not from any church or even from my own family.
I suppose my biggest fear is dismissal.
You always hear talk about "phases",
and as someone who has seemingly no solid foundations for what I feel,
that fear is all too legitimate.
I've never kissed a girl or even been in a proper relationship.

So the problem is,
how does one communicate a fact without any sources?
It's more difficult.
She'll ask, "Well, where's this woman then?"
and I'd rather avoid all that.

So should I come out now
or wait until I've met a girl
who'd like to drink tea with me

and watch bad TV.

A girl who's sweet enough not to cringe
when she reads my poetry,
and would not be opposed
to having sex in weird places

or drinking in quiet bars
that play The Rolling Stones.

And if you haven't dismissed me yet,
I promise to propose as soon as I get my car.

The Old House

Blackberry picking
Houses of cards
Arguments never heard
In the midst of pine
furniture everywhere
death lies on the door
What is endless but green?

I imagine that at night
all the leaves descend
over our earth
as to be removed like us
and the memories
which now buzz in knowing
of what would be lost in a year.

Now we drive by
and I am being informed
that my childhood home
has been filled with *Italians*
who once brought out the guards
have broken all the furniture
but most important of all

Don't even farm.

And I say, Sure it's nothing
the place hasn't seen before.

It's a joke, so we laugh,
but I'm thinking of how

easily one can divorce whole lives
from what once was a place of love

for some.

May I?

Summer's here.
Is this to be
another lonely year?

Sick of the birds and the bees,
give me my most bodily season
full of churning approaches.

To be truly introspective
is to leave it so
I have to mop the fluids.
On this occasion alone
do we prize what's been used,
so don't be afraid to get consecutive!

We might just turn to lovers
the second time around,
once sweat has dripped

gently off a nose
and rolled along the worn-out flesh
of some body's open road.

Leon Thompson

I was born in Dublin, although raised in Cork for most of my childhood before returning to Dublin where I have lived since. I go to school, due to sit my Leaving Certificate in June 2020 and hope to study in DCU, school and homelife was where I gained most of my inspiration to begin writing poetry.

Naked My coming out experience was not how I expected it to be to say the least and for a while I didn't have many words to describe how it made me feel. Which is exactly what I wanted this poem to reflect.

To Him Ironically, I strayed far away from trying to distance myself from this poem. I had a concrete idea of how I wanted this poem to sound as it was a direct address towards how my father made me feel the day I came out. Although it can easily be interpreted however someone pleases. **To Her** This poem also followed a purposeful disconnect as the universal problem of womanhood, abuse and family are something I expected a lot of people to relate to.

Honey I consider my humour to be sarcastic mostly so I decided to compare honey, renowned for its sweetness, to the bitterness of love. Simply. **Blotto** When I started writing poems, I knew I wanted them to be personal but vague enough for other people to read and relate to their own situation and hopefully help them to understand issues they might be going through but didn't have an answer to.

When i know i'll love you When writing this poem I wrote it from a different perspective from where I would usually approach writing. I knew what I wanted to express the same way I know what I want in my life, regardless of the length of time that may take.

naked

never did i feel exposed
until this moment

where words consumed body
and body consumed shame.

to him

Did you not think your lack of depth would hurt?
Intimacy seems like a chore and
Silk sheets will never be as soft as your words and
Analytical undertones that you breathe more than air.
Preciseness was your forte.
Please never mistake this for carefulness,
Omnipotent because i was a child,
Inferior because i was a different type of man.
New changes arent easy to come to terms with you say
Tempted to look but remained hard like your
Mission was elsewhere.
Envious of your ability to,
Never dwell long enough
To cry— you couldn't be a man then.

to her

By nature you learned to care and bare with
the hardships you dealt with even as a
child-
when drowned with problems from family
past and present, you kept the water
Calm. Still and a mystery like your
unspoken but voiced hurting
And it wasn't your kin that
Ensured justice was
provided to you.
You endured it too
Why endure the pain again
of silencing yourself and hiding
from the sun to bury a truth it always knew.
If I could give you back your childhood to sniff
lilies and not the berries I would in a heartbeat-

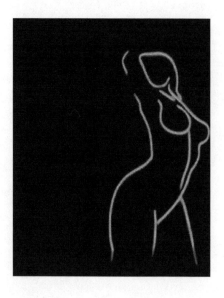

honey

loving you was not as easy as soothing
my throat with honey from the hive,
that enslaved lives to cure my hurting.

You were equally as sweet,
hard like toffee but not to the bite.
Complicated like honeycombs but not intentional.

My mother told me to take a spoonful,
did she mean of you too?
Should I savour the sweetness—
Could I would be more realistic.

blotto

it's an easy equation of feeling excluded,
you're either involved or you're not—

Everybody loves validation
and the honest satisfaction
from people's faces
when compliments are dished out
like coins at a church,
quickly pocketed by greed and validated by need.

if my confidence had grown from others-
would it or i have turned out differently?
i've had time to sit with it like most things in life-
i'll compare it to liquor, it's easy going down with the encouragement of
friends.
But when you're alone you still feel weak and sick.

My confidence was built by time and observation- as strong as brick
it was often compared to arrogance
and I had time to realise the difference.
if you're blotto from the admiration of yourself
but unaware of it,
your ego has outgrown you.

when i know i'll love you

what i need to survive is a not a kindling fire,
ignited by rage and fury.
i have an abundance of fire myself,
i am a target for the matchstick men and women,
that strike up ideals of love to burn anything different.

what i need to survive is a lily in the spring,
to balance the books,
and promise its bright colour will bring hope
instead of fear,
and that life will go on no matter how bad the losses.
I can feel good again.

we dont have to be opposites,
this is where a struggle appears for others,
Not many people can say this;
but i own the burden and pleasure of being self-aware of what i want, what
i need and why.

i keep my words vague in hopes of helping,
when i find you
and you love me—
help me understand why i will put you first in the future
and why i did in my past.
Make me feel okay with appropriate selfishness.

Méabh Ní Bhraonáin

Instagram: focaltosay

Writing has always been a passion of mine but only since leaving college, September of last year, have I had time to dedicate to it again. Inspiration comes from everywhere and anywhere but I find the best work comes when there's something of a story to tell. I'm still very new to poetry. I'm reading all that I can and trying to find my own voice and style.

The work I've entered includes a poem written during unprecedented times, one written during dark times, one of the most pathetic poems you'll ever read and one personal homage to a Greek tragedy.

New Normal

"Shall I pop the kettle on?" I ask my parents, for the seventh time today.
Every Irish person knows the cure: A nice hot cuppa *tae*.
While neighbours checked on neighbours, "D'ya have everything you need?"
And community came together, leaving no room for greed.
While pubs closed and in the process dried out the river made of green
And we witnessed the strangest Paddy's Day the world has ever seen.
While Facebook showed school children making their own parades
And we all got WhatsApp warnings from someone's Auntie Mairéad.

We waited for everything to go back to normal.

While work was done at home and there was more time for play
And every dog in Ireland was walked three times a day.
While football teams did food drives and dropped medicines off
And we prayed for every stranger with the smallest tickle of a cough.
Well, we let them hear that 203 was not enough to survive.
One little bee leaves just a sting, but they could not ignore the hive.
While those heroes scrambled to bend the curves and delay the timing
Of what no-one could have predicted would be a 2020 Easter Pining

Waiting for everything to go back to normal.

And soon the experts will say there's little and less left to fight.
Because we stayed together - but apart. Stayed at home and held on tight.
Back to work at the office in the jobs where you are skilled;
Will you once again look through the people who kept the food shelves filled?
Will the word hero still be donned to those in cleaning gloves and scrubs alike?
And will you remember who kept us going the next time workers strike?
Will the men in shirts say, in fact, 350 is much more than enough?
Will we stand together, just like now, and call them on their bluff?

When everything goes back to normal.

One thing's for sure, we'll hold our loved ones longer, tighter every day
And make sure the sincere 'Take care' stays around long after pandemic
goes away.
So I boil the kettle an eight time for, yet another, cup of tea
And ask my country, kindly, is this the new normal we need?

Hibernation

As sure as leaves fall gently to your feet
And the night falls closer and closer to morning,
So too, surely, will winter's arms come to take you.
She'll draw you indoors, promise warm embers and bellies.
Make comfortable your surroundings for the ease of Hibernation
And soon comfort itself will smother you
Till heartbeats become as regular as rustles from bare oak trees.
Winter will come to freeze you in time
And this invitation you must reject.

As meadows darken, lose technicolour and texture,
And the sun burns dimmer and dimmer each morning
So too, surely, fades the golden elixir that courses your veins.
She'll draw you indoors, safety granted in the settled slow.
Refuge, retreat, recluse, rewind.
Madonna pleads you rest. She pleads you sleep.
You cry. You mourn. You pause. You waste.
You slip through the storm that rages on.
You are sweetly cradled in her bosom till forgotten are any reasons
One would dare to mark the bitter sheets of snow.

Lupus, *Lupus*, they call *me* crazy!
They think my calls to the moon went unanswered.
But no triumph comes without challenge.
No hunt and kill without first starvation.
No.
I will not let winter's arms cause this climb to cease.
Muscles, senses, skills peak in summer's solstice.
I do not watch them atrophy.
I am the one who stalks the cold.
The one who fights the frost.
Wears the wind.
Hunts with hunger and
Sucks dry the marrow of the dead months.

103

I make my mark on the sheets of snow.

So,
When winter comes to freeze you in time
Will you settle for soft steady slumber
Or will you fight all instinct?
Face bone and blizzard.
Join me.
Hunt.

Howl!

Pathetti Spaghetti

There's a bowl on my bedside table
I don't know how long it's been there.
It looks like maybe it once contained pasta.
But I can't be sure and I kinda don't care.
I use half of my bed to dump stuff on
and the other half's for me.
Commuters on the quays tell me it's time to go sleep.
Their days are routine and regimented.
Mine: weeks long and utterly fragmented.
So, again, I draw the blinds.
Reclaim the night that's mine.
Four walls, laundry, a shopping bag that is now a bin,
Mess of chargers for laptops and phones and sin.
And I am yet to decide whether they exist to keep the devices or me
switched on.
All I know is that I've been *wired* to stay awake since she's been gone.

Here, I have lots of hobbies. Many ways to watch the days pass
I cover so many different topics without ever lifting my ass.
I can tell you far too much about cephalopods or how to restore vintage
Nike kicks.
I'm not proud, but I've seen all 10 seasons of Friends seven or eight times
on Netflix.
I even watch the show in French when I tire of reciting scripts
And listen to hours of pointless podcasts while doodling dogs.. or tits.
It's laundry day and I panic, I'm running out of clean underwear.
It's been laundry day for a week now and I panic cuz I don't seem to care.
It would be done today if I could just muster up the power.
Instead watch me do makeup, go to work and for a few hours
I forget the room so far away.
Shift is over, change clothes and then insist I stay
Out! All fuckin' night!
Drink, dance, trance, take a pill to feel new.
I do lots of things to distract myself now that I'm not with you.

Cuz wouldn't you want someone to see floorboards?
Would you look at the overflowing bin?
Mess, you confirm what I already know;
Nobody can come in.
Not yet. Not quite. Not until I clear all this shite up.
Reluctance in the form of spilt tobacco and a crusty coffee cup.
The last few bits and pieces of clutter
Left here to decay.
Stopping me from getting up or thinking I'm okay
I know what it is that holds me back.
It is the crippling fear
That when I show someone this room again
They won't even come near

To she,

To her,

To the before,

To the reason that a pile of clothes barricades my door.

There are some things, however, I am proud that I don't do
Like not reading old messages looking for old pieces of you
I'm proud of those deleted digits.
A lost lover's last lifeline.
The crutch I carried around with legs that work and move just fine.
So now I open up this space, once again, for me.
Books on shelves, clothes on hangers, possessor to be free.
Free to think. Free to sing. Free to dance. Free to laugh.
Free to say 'here, anyone coming back to my gaff?'
Because, after all, a problem shared is a problem halved.
Gas!
Guests!
Guess I'll pick up the pieces
Do it one step at a time.

Open up those bloody blinds
Reclaim the day that's mine.
And Surely. Slowly. I'll live the life I owe me.
Rid of empty chocolate wrappers and smelly socks and lonely.

I'll wake tomorrow morning and make both sides of the bed
And see no more pathetti spaghetti hovering above my head.

Turn Around

"Turn around" she asks.
But to turn around would damn us both.
This is our underworld.
It is no place for life.
Here, time stands still and so do I.
Still waters. Still breeze.
Still longing that which can't be seized.
Eurydice's fingers clasped around mine
Or is it just the ghost of the last time?
Either way, I cannot look back
To turn around would damn us both.

We do not belong here. Not where dead things lie.
Sisyphus strains, chained and tied.
Ever believing, non-conceding.
Push the rock. Hands, feet, bleeding.
Push the rock. Summit receding.
Push the rock. Reach the top.
Now, watch it tumble back to base.
No change to the tortured's face.
'Turn around' and *this* is our fate.
We do not belong here. Not where dead things lie.
Tantalus wades while he thirsts and wallows.
Shrunken stomach longs to swallow
The fruit overhead and just out of reach.
Memories – tangible, raw but sweet.
Flail out, in hunger, hands that never meet
Flesh divine;
Made like mine.
Taste in mind but never sated
Is this the way we must be fated?

For life is for the living.
These minds muddled with the gift of giving.

Giving meaning.
Giving feeling.
Giving hope.
Not stealing
From each other and from ourselves
In this perpetual circle of hell.
Get out! Get up! Get undone!
Climb from here and bask in the sun.
But the temptation,
Frustration,
Looking for some indication
that the other is just behind.
Must not look back.
It is with faith I climb.
Faith and Fate,
Faith and Fate,
Faith and Fate
That we might reunite in mortal state
because
To turn around would damn us both.

We are her and we are him.
You, my Orpheus,
Seamstress of word, of wonder and whim.
Lyrics embroidered from pen to paper
Thread, truth, tongue and twine through my thoughts.
I am,
I have been,
I will be
Naked before you
to look on with craftsman's eyes
Innate sense of shape and size;
When to cinch and to squeeze,
When to leave room to breathe.
Stitching form that binds me solid
and buckling weak at the knees.
So, clothe me, undress me, speak and impress me

with winded words, wrapped and woven.
Silk-spinning stories: silent and spoken.
Sing songs of lovers and those left heartbroken.
Now mend yourself
To someday open.
I cannot look back.
Goodbye was goodbye was goodbye and I
Will not roll the ball up and up the hill;
Will not reach for the fruit, and still,
"Turn around" she asked, and, in so,
I did it for me and
I did it for she; I said 'No'.
I did not turn around.

Mícheál McCann

is from Derry.
mmccann84@qub.ac.uk His poems
appear in *Poetry Ireland Review, The
Stinging Fly, Banshee Lit.* and *The
Tangerine.* He was a winner of the
inaugural Ireland Chair of Poetry
Student Prize in 2019, and is
featured on Poetry Ireland
Introductions 2020. His first
pamphlet of poems is forthcoming
from *Green Bottle Press* in 2020.

Mícheál McCann – I was really taken aback with the call for submissions
for a new anthology of Irish queer writers, realising how long it had been
since anything of the sort has been done. And in such a precarious period
of time too. I think it's a great thing you are doing. I'll not bore you with
many words about me, but I'm based in Belfast where I'm carrying out a
PhD on North American literature from the AIDS pandemic. . .

. . . The foundation of my thinking about poems is indebted to a few key
poets: immanence and the possibility of the present, Marie Howe and Mary
Ruefle; the sublime in queer life, Mark Doty; and many contemporary
writers from Ireland, i.e. (particularly) Colette Bryce, Sinéad Morrissey, and
Ciarán Carson. These poems are interested in tensions between rural family
and queerness, and there's a certain spiritual–if not theological–
extrapolation of grace within them. They're couched within the lyric poem
tradition, but are playful and maybe even frivolous or capricious, in others,
quiet and elegiac. Despite this, these poems are always convinced by the
possibility of queer joy, and in hope being excavated in the mire of the
immediate moment.

Apology

Sleep is not answering the phone
while the directors of our terrain
(we imagine them as coyotes
in carrot-coloured pant-suits)
ignore the line than runs red-hot
along the gated field by our house.
You, Fire Boy, lavish inside: the day's
sun knocks against your drawn curtain
and from the outside your room
flashes with strobe-bang! brilliance.
An Irish heat distorts the pavement
but fear not, you are building a city.
This room you game in. Your bolt-hole
was mine long ago but I lost the deed,
keep it, and keep your hands moulded
around what allows control of your world.
When I roar about reading or wild herbs
I only envy this wonderful new world
you craft, its crystal blue water, how
the villagers shout *Hail!* to everyone…
This world, built block by grassy block:
gold-brown truffles; fish leap the river.
Your brow is smooth, no tell-tale furrow.
I pull the curtain tighter, settle to watch.

Song

A-side

The streets
are hesitant
in these days
of illness.
You read poems
to a phone
in hope
of response.
Livestreams:
salmon leaping,
actors
acting?
boring weekly
vlogs (all seen)
of a pregnant
dachshund.
Something
here will
replenish
you surely.
A hairbrush
displays grey
hairs with black
lately. God

B Side

A mason jar
for coconut
oil is being
re-populated
with pecans,
chia seeds,
flaked
almonds,
assorted
granola, yoghurt,
and an empty
house's pleasure.
It is in
this quiet
—slicing grapes
that burst their
skin's boundary—
I am reminded
of launching
from school
to the only car
in the world.
Sweets in tissue.

A supine palm

Letter

You will be alive.
You will be alive
to all the music in the autumn's going.
You will remain alive
to all that music in her coming and going
– the wooden hair brush has hairy teeth –
You will know the living
and all their music and dancing and kissing
and the smell of your mother's hair
in the porcelain cabin by the green sea.
You will know their lives
but not while they're dancing and nursing
you and your lover weeping into bedsheets
red stones bud flowerly in the garden of the porcelain cabin
and the purple sky scratches its knees.
You will resign your life
to the waning quavers of a tree's hair.
Your eyes bladed as horn-rimmed comb teeth
that grow briny as they peer to the sea: green
and the sky feeling sore watches a garden grow violets
while a little boy sees friends meeting on the spiky beach.
You will learn this living
and the song of dog-dirt-shoes and glasses banging
all while brushing her hair with the treasured comb
kept safe on the pebble-grey porcelain dish.
And the sky turns as it does to mending itself
while the boy needs no mending, he sees two embrace
through the lens of bottle-green sea glass.
The field exhales, pierces its ears with helleborine.

Bin Lids

for Patrick Scullion

is what she'd call us babes
that's no hem of a lie. But

she's a drag queen that
does literary impressions

better than the writers
themselves. And glam

as fuck. Don't let her catch
you praising her though.

Under that pink-gel lamp
you'll be a puddle in seconds.

Just hold back your wonder
and let it resound in sound

afterwards: a flower waking up
in her hair. We're not well.

She'd turn, flaming with geg
asks me so she does: do you have

a gay da? but before I say naw
the bartender squeezes past

and the doors to Union St. fold
open into a Belfast summer

night that is coming. The air...
Even the wee stage awaits it.

Spray-On Jeans

Eros shook my
mind like a mountain wind falling on oak trees
— Sappho

Terracotta denim folds down me like water
skin that is there, and gone when disturbed.

Red leaves fall from two beech trees.
A curtain pulled aside. Your hands a lockpick

The caked muck drunk-sang back to the call
of some north wind's touch. Yeah. There.

The night opened its eyes to rain replenishing and we
were finished. Would soon rise for cold tap water.

The jeans around my ankles: them, too, exhaling
from that cold-drip tension we called separation.

Brother

where have you
        gone my pal
               in a bang of fire and hair
and wearing and tearing
        your stare is playing
               hide and seek
and is skilled but
        i find it i always will
               and even though
i am hiding from you
        after a fashion
               half behind the oak tree
out the back in Culdaff
        the sea's there!
               and the tire!
i am with my dear friend
        so you think
               and here is this for you
        to find sometime: me
               clumsy in things
but always here-abouts
        even when i am not
               even when we leave toothpaste
opened and oozy even when
        we drive our ma to distraction
               even when you don't know the truth
            yet
find me here. i'll stay until then.
        will be by the water.

MORRIGAN CHADAIN NÍ COILEAÍN
ARTIST BIOGRAPHY

Morrigan Chadain Ní Coileáin is an Irish writer and artist. They are best known for writing poetry and their work in Fine art.

As a poet, they write on subjects ranging from past experiences to feminism to queer identity. Morrigan splits their time living between Ireland and France and lives with their grand cats.

Before they started writing and painting, Morrigan experimented with various interests: design, editing, fashion.

Their true passion is the one they are doing now - being an artist and poet. But they are still very bad at biographies

CHILD

Hate me

Hold me down

Love me in a way that is
necessary But you fool no one

In my
destruction You
are reborn A
better man

And I am nothing at all
A haggard old fool
For/ever loving you.

All the hopes and dreams.
I had for you
That you wished from
me Did you want another
That is tough love

For you will never have
another I am wasted, spent,
aggrieved Foolish for wishing
you loved

Me
You leave and feel left
Even though it was I
Who stayed by your
side And truly

I can never leave you.

FAIRY FIRE

Rain melts from sky to canal
The lone girl

Standing before the swaying gondolas
She watches the dusk
Which crawls to embrace the sun
Warm fires fill the flowing streets
Her dress a swaying heavy comfort
Slinking to the side alley
Soft fingers grasping warm stone
She watches

The lady is here
The lone girl watches the solitary lady
Fires swell in tandem

With the girl's tingling excitement
The Mandragora rages beyond
Heart irregular with the lapping drums
A sweeping turn

Eyes meeting
The Silent promise
Brilliantly their cord burns

The lady steps, a first move
Electric, shooting, the girl rushes

Whirls of flow, up steps of marble fire
Promised by the sounds of footsteps
Ragged breaths
A sequestered courtyard

Awash with fairy fire and warm gamboge silk

The lady waits
The girl reclined at the door
A clink of a lock
A stop in eternity

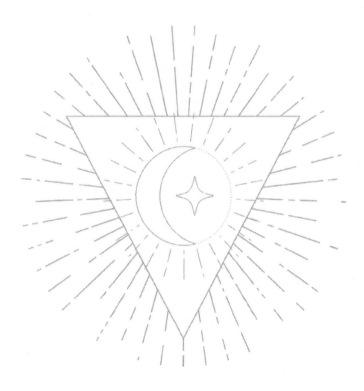

OF YOU

A drunken Lie
An angry
Word

Wishing to never see you again
What we had cannot be
mended I grieve for what once
was
For what you did for me

The gordian knot
Did my love for you change me?
Or did your affection enthral?

I could have been your
everything But you wished for
steel

When I was silk
You wished for bruises
When I offered blood

Where is that spark in your eyes?

Perhaps it was the slant of his
jaw That made his flaws
insignificant Mine too soft

And yet your chains never
loosened Your kiss poison in my
blood

Stop touching me
Wrong, Wrong, please stop!

Grief, it was not how I
hoped The moment mired in
shame A shell of an
experience With you

Cruelty is your nature, not
mine Never told you
The reason
unfathomable I accept
now
I should have
For me

Words that will never reach your
ears I wished to experience that
connection One more time
For the first
time? But not
with you I do not
miss you Only
the memory Of
You

THE WITCHING HOUSE

I am beguiled
      Ideally enraptured by the clearing in the woods
      Spectrum Violet flows in tandem
      To the dawning of the moon
      Within this dream sits a cottage
      Of glowing calm and lavender
      Queens Anne's lace embracing the curves of
      stone
      I am pulled

A cat's cry calling me home

RED BEAUTY

Screaming, I run

Wishing does not make it so

A striped Carnation,
withering, unwatered What's
the point, I think

Uprooted,
dying,
redundant
Just a
dying
pretty idol
A lobotomised life

Suffocated,
Screaming,
Useless
Why buy a
dying life
A
sic
k
sig
n
of
aff
ecti
on
Or
a
pro
mis

e

Looking
into the
dead deer's
eyes

I asked
why
Beca
use
she
was
beau
tiful
You
had
said.

I will not let you do the same to me

Orla Fay

from County Meath, edits *Boyne Berries* and *Drawn to the Light Press.* Recently her work has appeared in *Tales From The Forest, Impossible Archetype, Crannóg, Cyphers* and *The Lake.* She won 3rd place in The Oliver Goldsmith Poetry Competition 2019 and was highly commended in The Jonathan Swift Creative Writing Award 2019 and The Francis Ledwidge Poetry Award 2019. Her poem *The Natural Order* appeared in *The Irish Times* as a poem of the week in July 2019. Her debut collection is forthcoming from Salmon Poetry.
http://orlafay.blogspot.com/ Twitter@FayOrla

Radio Ga Ga

As the Barcelona Olympics unfolded over the summer
Freddie's duet with Montserrat Caballé aired on TV.
I would play the album over and over through those child-
to-teenager years of the early 90s. *It's a kind of Magic*
and *I want to break free* were anthems of too long holidays.
Under Pressure was also a track on Queen's Greatest Hits II,
the cd cover, black with the band's crest marked in gold.
Two fairies rest beneath two lions that hold a crown in a "Q"
on which a crab sits. All are in the wingspan of a phoenix.
Mercury created the emblem to represent the astrological signs
of the band members, two Leos, a Cancerian and a Virgo.
David was the spectre in the background, The Thin White Duke
who entered stage left in my early 20s when the shackles came off,
when I was more ready to meet a realer version of myself,
one no longer bound by expectations of peers, family, society.
I wanted to scream, to dance so hard my heart would fall out,
grow horns and hooves like the guitarist on *Dead Man Walking*
whom I had gasped at while watching an episode of Top of The Pops.

"Well Worth Doing..."

Recalling Marian Finucane's Interview with Nuala O'Faolain

She had been diagnosed with a terminal cancer
that began in her lungs, travelled to her brain
and then her liver. She would be dead in weeks.
She regretted smoking and drinking too much,
wishing she had taken better care of her health
and reflected more on this life. No longer caring
for Proust whom she had read in the Shah's Iran
she felt forsaken by the world that left her no treats,
no sense of appreciation for its natural beauty at the end.
Still a little music and food brought enjoyment,
the milky coffee and crusty bread in Paris,
Schubert's *Death and the Maiden* played by a string quartet.
She wondered what the point of existence was
in this going too soon, the unpreparedness,
the things only known by the self,
taken into the aloneness of the darkness?

I had read her memoir *Are you somebody?*
in my early 20s when I was struggling with my own identity.
It meant something to me, made a difference,
that courage she had in telling her story.
She whispered faintly at the end of the segment,
"It was well worth doing..."

Wildflowers

The walls fall on the place,
a folded-up room in memory, a doll's house
packed away for another generation,

or for now to take from the attic.
The Convent. A big safe community to grow in.
A garden where weeds were secrets.

The pruning discipline kept us in check,
mostly. At 17 and 18 we flourished,
freedom's burst could not be curtailed.

Anything was meant to be possible.
We were supposed to be roses and belles.
The hidden nettles appeared later,

along with untended, sticky cleavers.
Nobody had explained the value
of daisies, dandelions and buttercups.

A Red, Red Rose

-      after Burns

She was lovely as the rose
planted in youth's garden,
blooming in the summertime
as dawn birds were singing.

She cherished her dearly then
in the throes of romantic passion
never guessing how one day
she would be out of fashion.

She swore by letters to be true,
by lakes deep and mountains high
but she was a silent universe
granting no courteous reply.

Like Lancelot she let her go,
pining by eternity's gate.
In a past life she still loves Gwen,
but in this century, it is too late.

Green Book at The Odeon

Before the longed-for trailers
the adverts play and the neon
Odeon signs light the theatre.
"Switch off your phone, sit back
and relax!" I'm told by automation.
And I do. I relish the hideaway,
the getting away from it all,
the one to one connection between
the unfolding story and myself.
It is a pure thing, a soul connection,
a mirrored exchange of emotion.

In the deep South in the early '60s
there was a Green Book, a guide
with a list of establishments for 'coloreds'.
But bonds of humanity are made
when experiences are shared,
when time is spent together,
when love and friendship see
not with the eye, but with the heart.
What is it to know someone
if not to walk a mile in their shoes
to feel empathy, to unveil beauty skin deep?

Richard Kilian Neville

is a 22-year-old actor and poet from Cabinteely, currently studying European Studies in Trinity College. His work addresses family, sexuality, and politics.

Richard Kilian Neville – These poems were mostly written in Paris, France and performed in a small bistro called Au Chat Noir with some very special friends. They follow some realisations that cross your mind as you first step into who you are. Ideas like love and family became so painful to consider that you think they mustn't be for you.

They consider how scary rejection can be and how disappointing it is to take steps back when you can see a fulfilled person so near.

And finally, a kind of serenity when all the things that plague you fall away, and the way you feel doesn't seem so frightening.

133

A Ballad in Pink

The words seep from your lips like treacle
sticking to the sides of your teeth,
and muffling your words.
But you spit them anyway.

Your arms are folded tight
like you guard the gates
to neighbourhoods that I dare not step –
Places I grasp thrilling glances of to my belly.

Your pupils beg me to comprehend
what your mind conceived;
How you mind convulsed –
Seeing skin tight denim and fingernails
twirling in pretty circles.
They glint with the love
of a wooden spoon.
Your pupils open gaping like a scream,
like mine did.

When they regarded themselves –
When they saw the hands grasp one another
and heard the lips uttering chants to sacred heavens.
A tongue curling around the unfamiliar words of a song that begs
the Power in the air and the trees and the streams to rip it from you:
To baptise you in paint thinner, to hold your filthy palm and sand your
round edges with aluminium wool –

You need not utter one word.

I have held the glint in your eye
in the middle of my belly
and felt it sear my guts –

Felt it tighten my lips
and take away the wrinkles
from the sides of my eyes.
Felt it evaporate the stream of honey
that catches my breath
when I can hear his steady heart beat,
and mine slows to meet it.

I know what it is to cling to a hot mind
as you feel it seeping into sand.

Hands dig into each other
sharp as nails buzzing red hot –
As loudly as my head
circling like tepid tea down the sink.

Broken Heart

Why do they pray for the
sweet taste of fruit and the
fast and beautiful release
of warm summer mornings

Do they feel the air differently
than my skin does? Recoiling
at the sweet aroma of
fresh roasted beef, of fish.

When they press their palms
Together in union, regarding
Each other's eyes deep
Drinking their souls' quiet whispers –

Why do my hands feel so dry?
Why are they as solemn as sandpaper?
When I moisturize them daily
when I warm them on the fire
when I hurl them upon the altar.
Begging for divine word, for divine spirit.
To fill me up and sprinkle droplets of
salty water upon my tired face –
When my lips quench for the electricity in the air
as the season changes
my body trembles in anticipation
yet again.

Is my youthful and fretful mind
stuck upon my childhood mattress?
Or does my body not love
the way that bodies love?

Will the dirt eat my leather skin
as my blood drips in wet release?
Will my heart feel kind enough to open
to make my soft tears cease?

People Watching

Buildings four, five windows
high
holding little boxes that spill ivy.

Small stools which creak when
you sit
and green neon crosses which
flash.

How do the coats decide where
their eyes will look at their
various screens?

Where they will buy Granny
Smith apples
and fill boxes with crosses and
ticks?

Hair gets darker, freckles blend
and wash
away in the shower.
I know exactly what an espresso
is.

I scroll through the list of
beautiful things in my mind and
I'm not done,
But there are only a few pages
left.

You drag the razor across my
neck and run your finger on the
paper skin beneath
the lines on your forehead crease
and
the hairs on your fingers stand
on end –

You make pasta, I guess.
Twirling silver in your hand and
maybe –

There isn't a lot more beautiful
than a left hand that wraps
around tiny sticky fingers
and a right that carries a small
red bicycle.

First Date

The iron trembles in your jelly
hand
that can't quite grip the handle as
it smooths the wrinkles in that
shirt
you got on Amazon, on offer.

The shoes are the ones you wore
when you said thank you to the
florist
carrying a corsage and a bouquet
to the concrete where you
learned to read.

The window sparkles and you
turn
to see the Tower, dazzling –
A palace where only visitors live
and the king puts out the lamps
at 1am.

You want to know his tongue.
To make his teeth shine with
words
and catch his breath with how
you say
them –
To build stories with wit and
irony and intelligence.

You want to leave your
earphones
on your bedside desk.

To let the music that makes your
head full with song
be his voice –

To let your knees touch
when you sit next to one another
on the train,
To feel his glance
toward your glance,
watching platforms go by –

To see the steam from his breath
in the cold air
turn to the smoke of your first
cigarette –
I think he loves you –

I think he loves you.

You hang his picture beside the
canary in a cage
and look at it fondly. You lock
your bedroom door
the screen turns dark and the
eyes in your head
drink in the reflections of a
million faces and
your eyes meet –
But only through glass –
and they're filled with the same
Hunger.

You scratch the glass with your
nails
and you call to them
call as loud as your voice will
carry

and as sharp as your nails can
scratch
to make them look at you
you scream at them
till your throat is raw
till your fingers bleed
but they won't hear you
they can't hear you –

And the light's so white.
And frost tries to slip in
through the edges of
windowpanes.

Hands press pomegranates
against the mouth
and suddenly you're falling
falling hundreds of feet
your tiny tongue trembles
your lips wide open in a silent
shriek
your eyes glint and twist back in
your skull
till you topple onto a bare
mattress –

Your shoulders shrink and
your hair gets blonder and
your freckles sprout like tiny
saplings.

The Tower starts sparkling again.
And your hands grip for dear life
to the wet duvet.

And the trains are passing
faster than your mind can
comprehend.

Magpies

There is a lot of light
that breaks through
the low branches.

And a lot of foam
on top of warm
cappuccino.

The mountain head
glitters silver against
radiant mist.

There is laughter in the trees –
Laughter which tickles
your plump cheeks, instead of
mocking them.

Your hand traces the golden leaves
till they are tiny digits
and suddenly you are filled with childlike wonder –

Your breath mixes with the clouds in the sky –
Rising through the crisp air
and you float
and you float upon warm voices and kind words
gazing down, down with bright eyes,
That see fields passing like pictures in a film –

Birds writhe through the air
and the soft mouth of a boy
breathes that one is for sorrow,
that two is for joy.

Riocárd Ó hOddail (Richard Huddleson)

A lot of Ireland's queer history has been hidden away and denied to us. Now we have the massive task of uncovering and breathing life into that neglected past, pulling bodies out of the cold clay. As I sleuth my way through sources in the archive, trying to piece that fleeting past together, I realise that these people looking back at us have been actively silenced. There's very little written down about what they themselves made of the Ireland of their day and what kind of future they longed for. Frozen in time, they are still bodies on photographic film or subtle, ephemeral traces, like a fading handprint or a used condom lost in a landscape. In my work, I try to give these ghosts a voice, to imagine what they're thinking as they battle on through life.

When I look around Belfast and I see all the memorial gardens to fallen combatants and victims of the Troubles, I have to ask myself why there isn't a garden for those whose lives were cruelly cut short, such as Anthony McCleave, by society's own phobias. Cliché as it may sound, I want my poetry to act as a little garden for those thoughts and moments, and I hope that one day we will have actual gardens in the city to remember those victims.

I turn to the Irish language when I write these poems, mainly because there's a toxic assumption that queerness can only be articulated through English – and that's a notion I'm eager to derail. I'm always inspired by Cathal Ó Searcaigh's work, but I realise there's still a lot of ground to cover if we're to bring queer Irish-language poetry up to speed with what is available in other languages.

Sinsear aiteach

D'aimsigh mé do phictiúr
an lá faoi dheireadh.
Agus bhí an t-ádh dearg ort!
Ardoifig an Phoist.
Mí an Mheithimh, 1983.

Chas mé an leathanach.
Agus bhí cuma iomlán éagsúil ort go tobann.

Bhí tuirse ort.
Bhí tú ag imeacht as.
Bhí do chorp clúdaithe le cnapáin.
Ach bhí do gháire fós ann!

Codladh sámh duit, mo shinsear aiteach.
Maireann do ghlóir fós.

Queer Ancestor

I found your picture
the other day.
You looked so happy!
The GPO.
June, 1983.

I turned the page.
And you suddenly changed.

You were tired.
You were wasting away.
Your body covered in growths.
But your smile was still there!

Sleep well, my queer ancestor.
Your glory lives on.

An léarscáil

Tá léarscáil den domhan agam,
ach níl sé déanta as páipéir,
tá sé déanta as mo chorp féin.
Cneácha pianmhara,
meallta ailseacha,
cuimhneacháin shíoraí an ghrá

Focáil mé
nó tréig mé.

The map

I have a map of the world on me,
but it's not made of paper.
It's made of my body itself.
Painful sores,
cancerous growths,
eternal souvenirs of love.

Fuck me
Or abandon me.

Tástáil VEID

Cúpla ceist.
Snáthaid ghéar.
Lámha fuara.
Mo chraiceann.
Deoir fola.
A dhia na fírinne:
Nocht mo chinniúit.

HIV Test

A couple of questions.
A sharp needle.
Cold hands.
My skin.
Drop of blood.
God of truth:
Reveal my fate.

Impí

A leannáin,
Tá brón orm.
Tchím an t-aithreachas
i do dhá shúil ghorm.
Mharaigh mé an
Duine gan stoirm.
Fan ar mo thaobh.
Ciúnaigh an toirm.

Plea

O'Lover
I am sorry.
I see the regret
In your two blue eyes.
I killed the
Quiet man.
Stay at my side.
Silence the clangour.

S. H. Bramble

born November 2000, is a genderqueer writer from Galway who is currently studying English in college. He enjoys writing poems about love and being trans but is presently spending most of his spare time working on a fantasy novel. He solely writes in green biro because he feels they don't get enough love. S. H. Bramble wrote a one act play on the theme of diversity that received an honourable mention in the RTÉ Schools Playwright Competition in 2017. He thinks it is important to include queer characters in his writing and so draws a lot of inspiration from his own experiences as a queer person.

Night-Time Oaths

The strength in darkness isn't always the same in the sun.
It's easy to be proud when prying eyes aren't on you;
The blanket of night hides your blush and fear is tucked up tight.

One can stand tall and angry, determined to share the truth
While wrapped up snug with the support of the shadows
But in the warmth of the day a lie slips out,
Smooth as honey but nowhere near as sweet.

The bitter sticky residue lingers in my throat
And I want to take it back but it's too late —
My breathing is shallow and my heart is hammering.
"Next time," that weaselly voice in my head promises but we both know he
lies.

Lighthouse

I never imagined the freedom
That could come
From being in a room
Surrounded by people just like me.

To know we all chafed at
The gender assigned to us by society
And struggled to find the courage
To truly be ourselves,

Gave me a sense of peace
That I never experienced before.
The minority became the majority;
Confidence and power in numbers.

I drew strength from the ease
The others had in themselves;
I still feel like an imposter,
Tricking my way into masculinity.

They too were (are) haunted by the
Temptation of what should have been,
And the struggle to shake off that
Expectation like a wet dog in a dry room.

I cling to the blanket of normality
With shaky fingers and knuckles white with terror.
I don't want to tell the world that
I'm an actor just yet.

Let the audience enjoy the show a moment longer.

The Closet

Even now the feeling lingers,
Itching under my skin,
Memories of a different me.
I look back and wonder,
Who was she?

Did she ever exist at all
Or was she just a façade?
A character that I would always be.
Fifteen years I spent as her
Until I finally could see.

Even now that I know
I am shoved back into a lie.
Stopped from being me.
I am aware of the truth but
Still I am not free.

Inching my way out
Only to be shoved right back in.
But in that small room
I made friends galore
And started to bloom.

I might be content but
It doesn't make it okay
That the only place I am me
Is a figurative closet
Which encourages me to be free.

One Day

One day I will get to show you my house in the sun.
You will look on the fields and flowers
And trees with your own eyes
While my hand is clasped in yours.

We will walk down Shop Street
Under the grey sky,
Chatter about the bright shop fronts
And make a run for it when the sky opens.

We will live in a place
All of our own, that
Protects us from the outside world
And all its prejudices.

We will have a dog,
And a cat,
And at least 27 plants
Sitting on surfaces all around our house.

So that we trip over them
Every time we go somewhere
But we never mind,
Not really

Because it is ours,
And the furthest apart
We can be is
A four-hour drive down twisty country roads.

Grandad

It's hard to say that I'm sad
Because I barely remember.
Yet sometimes it really
Hits me
Exactly what I've lost.

In those moments I reflect
On the blurry memories
And bright photographs
Of my childhood;

Childish scrawl on a newspaper crossword,
Colourful lights, and giddy laughter
Around the dinner table.

Yet I cannot forget
Dark, wet mornings leading
Into January
And the feeling of dread that
Something wasn't quite right.

I hear the echo of a song
That makes my skin crawl and
Shop light flash by,
Guiding the way to where
I say goodbye, for the last time.

Unapologetically Queer

Our words were forged in
The blood
Of our ancestors, and
Over my dead body will I let you
Silence Me and My Words.
I respect
Your Pain,
But you must respect
My Anger also.

Time and Time
Again
I have been told that
Q*eer is a slur,
As if it's nothing but a Slur.
The same person conveniently
Forgetting
That g*y has been used in
The same manner;
That l*sbian has been seen
As a dirty word, a bad word;
That's it's those tr*nssexuals
Who ruin everything with their agenda.

Our words are not clean.
None of them.

So don't try and
Bury
One as a dirty secret
And canonise another,
When they have done the same thing,
Been used the same way.

I'm tired of it.
Tired of the same arguments,
The same fighting over and over.
We need to stop brawling
With each other,
And fight what actually matters.

S.J. Saighead

is a Kilkenny born, Dublin-based poet, playwright, and novelist. His work has previously appeared in *Poetry Ireland Review*, *The Honest Ulsterman*, *Mutability Literature*, *HeadStuff*, and *Hot Press*. He is currently working on his first collection of poetry and first novel, both exploring themes around queer life in Ireland. S.J. Saighead founded and edits the literary journal *Mutability Literature*, and online exhibition space *The Artistic Differences Project*.

S.J. Saighead – 'The Song for Him' is the culmination of my first unpublished collection 'Songs for Him'. The collection as a whole was an attempt to reclaim the pronoun 'him' in my work, which I had been avoiding up until this point, directing my love poetry at 'her' or 'you'. 'The Song for Him' maps out my developing sexuality through the lens of four key 'loves' during my youth to whom each section is directed. It reclaims the forms of epic, heroic poetry and lays bare the queerness of the subject, often hidden in subtext in many historical examples of the form. The second poem 'A Birthday Poem' is a short poem written for my boyfriend on his birthday.

The Song for Him

Ireland does not welcome that which is strange,
for years abnormal men loved out of range
of suspicious eyes and hateful glances,
they escaped from here given their chances.
The land of saints, of scholars, tales, and glee,
some stories were forgotten, never free.
O Gods of language this song is yours,
of stories lost discover open doors
which through one can enter a world once lost,
a world whose people, destroyed at any cost.
A world beneath all you did once know,
a world now stronger, starting to grow.
To claim a space beside those everymen,
who have new softened smiles, to welcome kin.
But fair Ireland persists in fear or doubt,
the balance of normal they can't go without.
Our heroes live in places such as these,
near towns and fields, out between the trees.
And here the story can begin; with boys,
and love, sordid and sweet. Infinite joys
these boys may greet. But fear, distrust, distaste
linger on and these are foes that must be faced.

I
A solitary mouse you crept into
his life. Beyond the realms of vision, you
began your journey. Faceless, nameless and
without a thought for care. You made a grand
entrance into our hero's lonely space.
Behind a locked door, his personless place
he started to explore his immediate
surroundings, through grey screens and texting late
into the night with men with dirty minds

156

and filthier phones. They search for meat like lions
do for a kill; the younger, the better.
He was but prey to some but you came after.
He first mistook you for someone he knew:
A farmer quite handsome, one of the few,
to own a heart as large as his farmland.
A joy his body evoked in him offhand
by meeting eyes or simply brushing arms,
but farmer's sons won't suffer these fair charms.
With mistrust and anger, greeted his inquest,
because he asked for your name: a brass request.
This stirred in you a feeling you knew well,
this sense of being stalked rung a bell.
But he was not a senile man, or your
demons who waited for sin at the door.
After the act of caged dog had ceased,
your mind and love recognised this feast.
For you and him each day was just a wait
to come home and check the messages late.
From you to him and him to you. You knew
wonderful surrender to that which is true:
He loved you despite you hating this
which gave you the ache witch hoped for his kiss.
In darkness both you and him overjoyed,
discovered love somewhere in a void.
Beyond the world of the zero and one,
You learned that this could not be proved wrong.
As time progressed you grew more brave. And call
you did upon the phone. Against a wall
you pressed your body, trying to forget
everything but him and you. He had met
all expectations, words fell from your mind
into his mouth, as you began to find
a feeling previously to this unknown:
with him you felt safe. You had outgrown
Your Father's rage, your Brother's fears, and your
own denial. This love you knew was sure.

All night you talked, all the while he saw
your future beside his own one. No flaw
he saw in his own master plan, away
you two could run, to love as you may.
Your body and his body connected
by waves, could touch at last unaffected
by the secrets you kept. But moments end
as do grand gestures, you could not pretend
now anymore, as much as you'd like;
this was a balance you could never strike.
You loved the country, family, him. But he
was not worth giving up two of the three.
So never did you meet your love. His touch
you never felt, his lips you never brushed.
He was a dream on a screen, nothing more.
Now if he called you would ask him what for.
He wondered sometimes, if that was the end.
He stopped when he saw you had girlfriend.

II
You were in his class for many a year,
before something had changed and brought you near.
So after ten odd years of passing face,
friendship developed and began to place
the seeds of want or something else, inside
his brain. So, quickly never was he outside
your shadow. This you did not try oppose
like you he would stand outside of those
which nature blessed with body and wit
on fields and off, a light you did not fit.
You laughed together and enjoyed the peace
companionship did bring, this did increase
in him a love he had not known in quite
some time, a love beyond he could not fight
though try he did in order to save your
own feelings and his. But this was before
you had begun to tease his lust with jokes

158

and comments off-hand, designed to provoke
reactions that might give a sign or hint
to his own persuasion, to which it didn't.
But both did know and neither could admit,
their friendship was now growing bit by bit,
into something you did not understand
and feared your feelings would get out of hand.
But still you continued to mess about
till he was in love, a believer devout;
The Church of your soul, body, and behind,
as close to perfection as he could find.
So every Monday before any games,
you'd change with him, without any aims
bar making him desire every spot
of skin you possessed but touch he could not.
So slowly you'd lose every inch of cloth
and watch with delight when he would get caught
in the world constructed by him for you;
a world occupied by barely a few.
Where you could live with him without a care,
to love and hold him, a world you could share.
You see this happen, through his eyes you know
if you want him you could let this love grow
or kill it right there, right now as he stands,
as he tries not to look and wrings his hands.
Your body was grand, a statue designed
by the old masters to turn mortals blind.
Your skin soft and clear, begging to be touched;
When you were made, God was not in a rush.
Your elegant fingers, a chest as wide
and strong as a jungle river. Denied
of this you drove him mad with hope and lust,
he was then yours, but even love can rust.
There's only so much loss one's heart can take,
especially when it knows love is fake.
And though to him, you look as lovely now,
a passing glance is all he will allow.

You fooled a friend to lover's submission,
a state he left of his own volition.
But only when he left did you then see,
all that you wanted *was lying with he. . .*

III
. . . You met and at once you both somehow knew,
that he was the one, the one of a few;
who saw past the skin, past the bone and meat,
whose rhythm your own would not have to compete.
The words shared between you felt familiar,
he could define your thought without failure.
You found in him what he had found in you,
a foot that would always fit your odd shoe.
And love consumed you as water consumes,
at once and completely, he found the rooms
that you had kept locked for fear of judgement,
but he saw all this and knew what they meant.
He knew you were one who gave everyone
something, till bit by bit all of you's gone,
except those locked doors whose keys were your own,
but you let him in so neither one was alone.
And though you lay asleep so far away,
you know that this love will never decay.
Because when his name appears on your phone,
it pulls you out from the depths of unknown;
with light words flung with archer's precision,
providing life a brief intermission.
You know in that moment he means to you
more than the land that separated you.
And when you meet though long it could have been,
you act together as though it's routine.
His soul and his person compliments yours,
so neither is strained and the love endures.
But this is not love of the king sung before,
this is the love that will prove to endure,
because this is not as Eros commands

this is love for which all and no gods stand.
You do not see this man as your lover.
He considers you closer to him, a brother.

IV
You came at a time when all was not lost.
The ices of youth had begun to defrost;
And in the run off water fear and doubt,
these things he had begun to live without.
And in you came like a mole in the gang,
but he could not silence the bell you rang.
So half a moment into his new life,
you walked in smiling and introduced strife.
You should have known from your toes to your lips
was enough to throw him into the grips
of impossible lust, of want for you,
but once again there was nothing to do
except sit and hear your mouth pour out sound
as he sat and listened, watching the ground.
For weeks he sat engaged in despair,
he mourned every moment you were not there.
But closer you grew, through reading and talks
and some long trivial afternoon walks.
Till one odd night he decided to chance,
and in one sharp movement began this dance.
Because on that night he found in your arms,
a strength and warmth that silenced alarms
that had begun to sound around his head
and in the quiet his mind had been made:
Your love was all he could ever need.
He was waiting to see where this would lead.
But he did not know that inside your head
something had emerged, something that you'd dread.
As the fire between you and him took hold,
so did the doubt that grew inside like mould.
This was not you, this was a foreign land.
But he had brought you here, led by the hand.

161

And closed in a box, behind all the fear;
you knew that somehow you liked it in here.
So on the second night, he asked again,
Again you indulged to love our King Wren.
But mould does not fade from the plasterboard,
When not seen, it's easily ignored.
After two nights of thoughtless abandon,
You had to leave your thoughtless companion.
It was all grand when it was fun and games,
but then people saw it, gave it their names.
And so you cut loose, though friends you remain;
a side of yourself from which you'll abstain.
And though you forgot, his love did not die,
but ask if that's true, he will surely lie.
He cannot blame you, for finding the door.
If that was an option, he too would ignore
the feelings he has for his fellow man,
he'd kill it before it even began.
Before all the pain, the shame and, the hate.
Before he knew what it was is innate.
Before he was gay, before he was gay.
Remember the day, remember the day.
Before this storm, before skies were grey.
He remembers fondly
                              before he was gay.

A Birthday Poem

for Rob

You find such joy in the night,
And bliss upon the morning.
You refuse me when I try to fight
And praise me without warning.

You tell me that you're lucky,
But I'm the one who's blessed;
In you I found a buddy,
And all my hopes expressed.

So here upon your birthday,
I want you now to know:
Never shall I go away,
To you my heart, I bestow.

You have it now forever,
So hold to close to your own,
And whatever be the weather,
You'll never be alone.

S. Nix

was drawn to the escapism offered by stories from a young age. Keenly interested in literature and film, she graduated with a Bachelor of Screen Arts from New Zealand, before returning home to Ireland. She spends most of her free time either animating or writing. She is interested in art's capability to capture and emphasise the mundane moments of life, and the emotions that make those moments stand out. Her work aims to reflect this, and often deals with themes of relationships and self-reflection. S. Nix writes poetry to try to help herself make sense of her world.

The featured poems all began to be written around the final stages of S. Nix' first long-term relationship, throughout the break-up, and into the period of reflection afterwards. This period was during the stage in her life where she began "coming out" to a wider group of family, friends and acquaintances. Therefore, themes of relationships, love, repression and fear feature heavily in the poems selected.

The Thrown Spear

I caught a thrown spear once;
Crisp catch, skin splintered,
Bitten in the bud before my chest was pierced
-Or so I thought.
She threw surer than I'd anticipated,
Leaving my hands bruised by reaction.
And, 'though lance-point never punctured me,
My once-blooded palms still bear her scars.

Pause

There's a Pause, in my head, who holds-
'Tis a cage/ from within/ I can't grow.
Although mellowed; when sunlight dissolves,
this bare-babed body recedes to shadow-
urged by a gurgle infantile in tone...

I censored, for so many years, that
'Though older, I still shoulder the habit of this fear.
And while I now know past-absorption is clear
What once I had buried, ferments, insincere.
There's a Pause-
in my head;
She ensnares.

Untitled

We wordlessly lay
With hands webbed 'tween us-
Our spines were s t r e t c h e d; Spread -
toe
to
crown.

In
      That
               Spacious
                           Instant,
I felt like a queen-
As if
this galaxy
was spawned
just for me.

Walls

The walls breathe in towards me
Nearing, like the lurching boards of a ship cabin caught in a storm.
Violent in their oppression, they push, and confine I.
Orbed in my eyes, they evolve and magnify,
consuming
Like a morphing 'mare, and I, trapped as a hare, am
unable to breathe.

So, enveloped, I assimilate!
...And become The Wall-
Turn'd taut and rigid with restraint.
No gasp, no wheeze, my locked grimace clings 'pon lips who rest, freezed-

One Sentence Out

One sentence out-
Reads the space between your words, and mine.
I pose the question in the form of an answer
And you respond on tangent-skewed.
It's less a conversation
Than a joust.

But
Within our sweet sparing
We speak quiet truths.
And admit, in jargon-jittered,
what the other had assumed...

So although every whisper is one sentence out-
With each new expression, we're growing.

Shipwreck

You are my Mast,
I, your Anchor.
But our ship leaks beneath tempest-torn sails.
So I must break my tether;
Hoping a careful current collects,
and carries you towards softer shores.
Because the dirge of our love howls failure
like a salt-choked machine,
And the swell-crash has splintered my heart,
And yours-

Yours drags,
Submerged by the Surge.
Don't let this anchor pull you to drown.
You're a warship, Her Majesty's.
Sail

The Dame of Damnation

A fogged-fatigue surrounds us; shroud-vision,
As Earth's fading clock tick-tocks, time-ticking.
Humans endure as though worker-ants; they follow worn paths, aim-lacking.

But;

I've heard tales of winged-witch who flies in, fleet,
her gaunt back garbed 'neath a cloak of defeat.
She jeers our fear luring us 'til ensnared; guilty or guiltless, we're hunted.

Thus;

Reaching blight-hands', dripping doom, lift our veil,
A tinnitus cackle shrills, dimming ears frail.
Next lunging, then plunging, with a blade now unsheathed,
the old crone will croon coolly as we fade...
-And be beat.

And then,
The fog will be sorely lifted.

And hence,
As we know it, time won't exist.

And so,
Life/ will dissolve/ beyond memory...

And now? -

Sam Ó Fearraigh

Sam grew up in Gort a'Choirce, Co. Donegal, where he recently returned after two years working in Spain. He writes poetry, short stories, and non-fiction, as well as scripts for stage and screen. He has worked as a theatre director, and has also taught English in Ireland and overseas. Despite being raised in the Gaeltacht, he spoke very little Irish until adulthood when he was drawn back to the language and began to study it seriously. In 2017, he earned a masters in Modern Irish from NUI Galway.

Sam Ó Fearraigh – Irish-speakers are often labelled 'enthusiasts' in a way that people who speak other languages are not. Who ever heard of a Portuguese or Mandarin-enthusiast? Ask an Irish-speaker, however, and they'll tell you we are a community, pobal na Gaeilge.

Being part of the LGBTQ+ community taught me how to feel at home in my own skin and learning Irish helped me feel at home in my own mind. As a queer poet writing in a minoritised language, I do sometimes feel doubly out of place. Nevertheless, Irish remains, fiercely, the language of my queerness, my language of inclusivity and belonging.

Fáinleog - Swallow: this poem was written in memory of my friend Clément, who would come to Donegal from France in the summertime when I was a child.

Balbháin - Mutes / Stutterers: this portrait of my father's parents is about events that happened before I was born, which nonetheless had a profound effect on my life.

Tá crann giúise ar imeall an chaoráin - There is a fir tree at the edge of the bog: a much less optimistic poem I wrote soon after moving back to Donegal.

Márta - March: I looked out the kitchen window and found this poem sitting in the back garden.

Dán Grá - Love Poem: I wrote this the night before the marriage equality referendum in 2015 – the first time in my life I felt I could, had to, wear my queerness openly.

Fáinleog

do Clément

Bhíodh muid ciotach ar dtús i dtólamh
i gcéadlaethanta an tsamhraidh
tar éis aon mhí dhéag de neamhaithne, tú

gan focal Béarla
gan bhaol ar an teanga
nár labhair mé ach leatsa.

Bhí eadrainn cairdeas
nár bunaíodh ar fhocla
ach gníomh. Charbh fhada

nó go rachadh muid caillte
i ndufair bheag na coille
gan againn ach dánacht is claíomh

adhmaid. Dhreap muid gach binn
i sliabhraon na hArdadh Móire
ag cur iontais ar an eallach

is nuair a d'fhágtá, cé gur bhrónach
an scaradh, fós bheifeá ar ais,
ar nós fáinleoige, sa tsamhradh.

– tháinig litir anuraidh ó do mháthair mhór
blianta ó d'imigh is nár phill tú, mí
nó dó i ndiaidh do ghnímh,
na focla lom: *Clément est mort* –

Ní cuimhin liom
caidé a dúradh
an t-am deireanach.

174

Slán sciobtha
a bheadh ann,
bhí muid óg

bheifeá ag pilleadh.
Thit críoch
i nganfhios orainn

agus an ghrian
ag éalú: slán
b'fhéidir, *adieu*

agus beagnach fiche bliain.

Balbháin

Seo chugat dhá phictiúr ón tsaol a tháinig romham –

Mo sheanmháthair ag cúlchaint
ina cistin bheag i nGlaschú
beag beann ar a cuid páistí
nach bhfuil a teanga acu.

Mo sheanathair i dtollán
á thochailt sna Garbhchríocha,
fir ag déanamh magaidh
fá chiotrúntacht a Bhéarla

Ach níl aon mhaitheas i bpictiúir
gan sonraí, cuirimis leofa –

Nuair a thosaigh mo sheanmháthair
mar chailín aimsire i nDùn Èideann
bhí uirthi litir a sheoladh. Chuaigh sí
amach ar an tsráid is d'aimsigh
bocsa, ach char shroich an litir
aonduine. Bhí mearbhall uirthi
óir chuartaigh sí go cúramach
an piléar ar a raibh *litter* scríofa
go lom sóiléir.
                    Fear trodach
a bhí i m'athair mór, tanaí ach gasta,
char ghlac sé le masla riamh, ach labhair
le dorn nuair a theip ar a teanga – bród
as ar dhíol sé le fostaíocht
is sláinte.

Stróic mo sheanthuistí an bhéalbhach dá mbéala –
ghlan siad a sceadamáin le sáile,
cha mbronnfadh siad gobán ar a sliocht

ach anois, is é muidinne atá balbh.

Tá crann giúise ar imeall an chaoráin

a bhfuil a chuid sciathán ardaithe aige
ag bagairt na spéire. Balbh,
cuireann sé m'athair mór i gcuimhne
domh – an chuma leathfhiáin chéanna,
garbh óir ba gharbh a bplandáil
anseo idir cnoc agus cladach.

A chrainn dhíl, a sheanathair, abraigí
an mar seo a fhásfas mise –
seargtha is folamh
idir breacuisce is sáile?

Márta

sabhaircín faoin bhalla –
bratach bheag bhuí
nach raibh ann inné,
nach mbeidh ann amárach

ag fógairt, ar nós tairngire
i bhfóram glas an gharraí
do dhuine ar bith a éistfeas léi,
theacht an earraigh.

Dán Grá

21 Bealtaine, 2015

Ghlac mé i mo bhéal thú
go bhfaca tú réaltaí úra
ag pléascadh thar imill na hoíche.

Dhá cholainn the
i bhfuarsholas gealaí –
gealach fhuar bhuí

dár mbreathnú le héad
frí fhuinneoga tanaí –
ba chuma linn.

Tháinig an codladh
agus ise á bá
go ciúin ins an aigéan laistiar dínn.

Bhí troime do chodlata
fáiscthe i mo sciatháin
is gile na maidine

ag sní fríd an spéir
amhail seanchneá á cneasú
den chéad uair ariamh.

Shia Conlon, b. 1990.

makes work centered around marginalized voices and about growing up in the landscape of working class Catholic Ireland. They have exhibited in London, New York, Dublin, Helsinki, San Francisco amongst others. Their work has been published in *The New York Times, i-D, Dazed and Confused* and in *Pilot Press Modern Queer Poets* alongside CA Conrad, Eileen Myles and more. . . .

L

after your death the crows came
they descended on our place
with white jackets and stethoscopes
they unravelled you from the wall.
i kept thinking
here she wept and here she sang

after your death i had to sit down
i sat for so long the government changed
they rewrote the constitution and now there was a cure
i kept thinking
here she wept and here she lived

after your death i began telling everyone you were murdered

skin

a mild bit
suitable for mouthing a youngster
puppy
foal
where i'm from
we begin at communion

nest

how did the body survive?
it undertook various journeys,
from one place to another.
it moved as its assigned role,
fluidly.
wearing sheer things over smooth skin,
it submitted to the will of God,
it submitted to the will of the couple
it flew into the hole in the wall, and stayed there,
throwing its wrappers out to the world
when it finished eating

workers

what to do with this body?
this life?
you almost left
until you heard the snap of fingers in the dark
you remembered those things called 'moments'
and that they are something to share
and that they could happen again
in places that smell of moss,
where we become factories for feelings,
we extend to each other;

               care,
               labour,
               dreams,
               a touch of the hand,
               a look of the eye

FENCES

i put a brick through it and it held up
death to all names not chosen
death to all houses
death to all diagnoses
i put a knife through it and it wouldn't die
death to all clocks
death to all family planning
death to all assignations not chosen
i spit in the face of it and it laughed
while we try sleep off our pills
it's making plans for our futures
on the day of our remembrance
the perfume ads become gender neutral
i put a bullet in its head and it didn't even notice
all my friends are waking up
they're saying death to all names not chosen
someone told us it dies only by water
so we're on our way
with pints and pints and pints
it's gonna choke, go under
then we'll sleep a sleep so natural
yeah
death to all assignations not chosen

Úna Nolan

is a 19-year-old word lover from Dublin, Ireland. As a child she was rarely found not absorbed in a book, and growing up she found a passion for communicating her feelings via the written word. Poetry has been a large part of her life for several years now, and she continues expressing herself through it. Úna Nolan has been previously published in *Crossways Literary Magazine*.

Úna Nolan – These poems explore love in its different forms. Love as it sours in divorce. Love in its first discovery, the overwhelming anxiety of realising perhaps this is not the kind of love that has been expected from you, or the kind of love you expected for yourself. Comfortable love, the sweetness of everyday when it cushions you. Broken love, the kind that lives to haunt and madden you.

BITTER

Oh my sweet, my candy-shaped heart in grubby child's clutching
Claws. My skin is twitching, itching, away from my vivacious veins
And bursting blood vessels. Purposely pull my peaceful mind from
Restful chest.
Rip all of me, each inch from soaring, souring romance. Our bed sheets
Are sharp now, each breath takes my soft skin and slits it open.
Tear the shared breaking of awful organs.
A victim of the vulnerable,
you made me nothing but.
I am pointless and precious to your
Arrogant infinite. How can I hope to heal the wanting?

But still, this is not just yours, blame is shared, ownership equal weight on
Our shaking, shivering shoulders.
The lawyers will swoop and vent the vulture's need across
Both our careless carcasses. Court rooms carefully strewn with
Two lukewarm coffees (they don't know your favourite, latte, extra hot).
Daring, darting glances of broken souls.
All that pleading purpose in
Languages we have always failed to translate.
We are obliterated, undone by all that unsaid.

Bitterness lays, a fine ash, over our whispering rubble of first dates
And shared hates, poisoned passion nights and
all that tender in the palm of our hands.
Your mother's first embrace, my fevered forehead calmed by your cool
Palm pressed to feel the rhythm in my chest.
Beating, beating, beating for you.

BEFORE

There's an enchantment entwining, defining, enlightening each step I take
To break the terrifying tension that spreads through this house.
This house so carefully built with loving limbs and kissing lips
Soft words and secret smiles,
Looks that seemed a glance but each held a hundred words unheard, insecurities
And infinities tied up in one universe that was all of him and her.
House once hushed, careful doors eased closed and babies on knees
Containing all the worlds adoration, perfection in four walls.

Now, a different silence shatters windows with its loudness.
False equivocator, act so well you can fool yourselves temporarily.
Silence is your stage; avoidance is your actors. You craft the perfect play to
Persuade yourselves (and no one else but you) that the encore must ensue.
Pretend eyes still look the same, that all-consuming emptiness
has not imploded through you
And filled you full with icy anger.
Four walls containing only one past, endless roads not taken. Sacrifices engraved
In concrete and red paint,
dreams drowned in marbled bathrooms and bitterness
Polluting every
Single
Inch.
I watch and I learn, I am shaped, and I am formed.
There is such perfect peace
In leaving these walls.
Set me loose, escape, evade, avoid.
Away is open and overwhelming.

HONEY

There's a bumblebee who sleeps at Little Lane
On that flower bush that's pink,
Where we used to sit and rest our heads
Blend bodies into earth and sink.

The pollen sits gleaming on six shiny legs
A drone of a buzz in our ears
You're nervous and shake as you watch my lips
Throat dry, you can taste all your fears.

I see dresses and skirts in the burn on her legs
(Skin tender and eager to flush)
We are youth and young and yearning
I move closer as blood starts to rush.

With no eyes the tension sits curved on my spine
Hearts faster with lines to be crossed,
The moons only voyeur to dark silence and secrets
A memory always living, yet lost.

I've tasted honey cradled in your collarbones
(I wonder if the bees come to visit)
My lungs, they need you to be whole,
But my God, there is pain to be different.

ROUTINE

Cold hand is refreshing and wakens my skin
The window is open to let morning in
Birds welcome my yawning and sleep-filled hello
Your smile tastes like sunshine, don't let me go.

Breakfast routines fade to coffee-fuelled exit.
I slipped food in your bag- I knew you'd forget it.
 The song on my breath has chest in a flutter
Compliment strangers to see the blush and the stutter.

The walk to the bus never feels quite so far
When the sun goes to bed she kisses the stars.
My body's most useful when it brings me to you
Don't worry. All's good. I'll be home soon.

CONNECTION

You have become the heaviest chapter in this book.
The safety of a childhood home once so familiar, familial,
Now nothing but a nerve needling glance out a car window on
A dull, daily drive.
I keep my vision fixated on the fleeting road
I am terrified of all that exists outside of my eyeline, my mind
Becomes my own horse's blinkers- protecting the perverse from me
And me from it.

But Oh, all that was once a sleep-heavy stumble down,
two stairs at a time
every creeping Christmas that actually felt like Christmas,
You corrupted it all in the walls of a whole new world.
Water falls on the windows and each rainfall washes
the last traces
of me
away.
There is a changeling in the mirror.
You spoil each note in the songs I used to sway to for
My own private moment, embracing the air to my lungs for the utter
unbelievable of us in my heart, in my phone,
 in my sheets.
But now words are wicked and never ending
When it is too late to be awake
Yet- my mind is hooked on every inch.
 Hit me again, again,
Again.
I'll take each one just feel the connection.

BLANK CANVAS

The artist draws his pristine, precise brush to
Bare canvas. Naked canvas. Exposed.
His work is controversial, universal, makes
Hearts stand-still.
Nervous and knowing. Scared of showing any inch
Of evidence of the moments yet to come.
But they will come.
Stealing hands, dirt-encrusted nails
Soil that is cold and trails, slither leave shivers
To run races from arch of back to shoulder curve.
Forever preserve infernal heat where hand printed
Permanent, permeating dirt.
Mark my mind into madness, sadness.
All the overflowing emotions, every rainbow colour.
Oh, careless creator. Write your story on my skin and
I will watch my body from across the room
For all the nights to come.
Paint me small, paint me silent
Paint it painless and let me forget it.
Does the canvas ever truly want to be created?